THE ART OF THE PLAYWRIGHT

THE ART
OF THE
PLAYWRIGHT

CREATING THE
MAGIC OF THEATRE

William Packard

PARAGON HOUSE PUBLISHERS

New York

Published in the United States by

Paragon House Publishers
90 Fifth Avenue
New York, New York 10011

Designed by *Paul Chevannes*

Second Printing

Library of Congress Cataloging-in-Publication Data

Packard, William.
    The art of the playwright.
    Bibliography:
    Includes index.
    1. Playwriting.   2. Drama—Technique.   I. Title.
PN1661.P3 1987   808.2   86-30369
ISBN 0-913729-77-9
ISBN 0-913729-62-0 (pbk.)

This book is dedicated to S. Barnitz Williams,
who taught me Senior English at Hebron Academy
in Maine and who encouraged me to write every
day of my life.

CONTENTS

FOREWORD

William Packard says that this book "tries to speak to both the serious playwright and the serious playgoer."

To the serious playwright who is young, still serving his apprenticeship and learning his craft, *The Art of The Playwright* will outline the bones of technique over which he can drape the flesh of his art.

And if the seasoned and experienced (and therefore very serious) playwright is anything like the rest of us, he will never cease to learn, to rediscover the things he has known all along, and Mr. Packard may remind him of some of them.

When it comes to serious playgoers, I suspect that most of them enjoy the theatre in the way that most of us enjoy music: we are basically ignorant about the very thing we are enjoying. The delight I derive from music is tempered by the knowledge that my gratification would be greater if I could listen with an informed and subtle ear.

Similarly, although your average playgoer (and for the purposes of this little homily let us pretend that such an "average" creature exists) is neither insensitive nor unaware, he nevertheless comes away from a dramatic performance not thinking (saying) anything much more substantial than "I had a really good time" or "I found it very moving (amusing)" or the vague equivalent thereof. I submit therefore that the enjoyment of any work of art is increased by familiarity with the technical processes of creation, and William Packard's book surely will be an exciting guide to anyone who wishes more fully to participate in the theatrical experience.

Alfred Hitchcock liked to refer to actors as "just children" (despite his inability to practice his profession without them). And in theatre circles it is common knowledge that more than one playwright has wished his plays could be performed without actors. Similarly, actors have been heard to mutter that they prefer to perform the works of playwrights who are either dead or at least somewhere else at the time of the performance.

Given this uncomfortable symbiosis (Webster: "the relationship of two or more organisms in a close association that may be but is not necessarily of benefit to each"), I am not unaware of the incongruity of an actor writing an introduction to a work on playwriting. My justification for performing this implausible task is that from the first time I stepped on the stage I perceived that I was an interpreter and not a creator, that without me the play went on, whereas without the playwright I could not go on. If *Hamlet* had never been performed it would still exist as a play, but no actor can act who has not been given words to speak. First comes the play, and only then comes the actor. It is in this spirit of unaccustomed humility that I pay tribute to *The Art of The Playwright,* a book which clearly and usefully explains the mechanics of creating something that makes it possible for me to earn a living.

José Ferrer

One of the most versatile actors ever to work in the American theatre, José Ferrer won an Academy Award for his performance in Cyrano de Bergerac, *and is also known for his performance as Toulouse-Lautrec in* Moulin Rouge, *and his direction and starring role as* Dreyfus. *Equally at home on television, film, and stage, Mr. Ferrer scored an early triumph in his interpretation of Iago to Paul Robeson's* Othello, *also starring Uta Hagen as Desdemona.*

PREFACE

From Neil Simon's advice to himself, ". . . Write slow but tear up fast," to George S. Kaufman's injunction to Moss Hart (*Act One*), "Just think about the bare bones baby," to Walter Kerr's instruction to everybody, "How Not to Write a Play," people have been telling people about playwriting.

Now Mr. Packard has written a new book on "The Art of the Playwright." I immediately suggested he retitle the book. I don't think it's modesty on my part to assert that there is no such thing as the Art of the Playwright, just as there is no such thing as the Art of the Director. Playwrights have skills as do directors but all of these skills relate to the creation of the theatre event. The art we all serve is the art of the theatre and it is a composite art. Authors, actors, directors, designers are all its practitioners.

Despite its title, I liked Mr. Packard's book because it was good to be reminded that we who practice theatre art have to practice it pragmatically. The most often asked question in our rehearsal halls is: "does it work or doesn't it work" and, of course, if it works, don't fix it. I at first was reluctant to say such an obvious thing, but after some thought decided it is fun to say an old thing, marred though the fun is by the knowledge that the message has already been delivered.

What one needs in this situation is the reassurance that we have freshly-eyed, poked and prodded it and come up with something usable. Mr. Packard has done this. Then by all means let's state it. State it with august gratification. Roll it off the tongue. Announce it in the manner it deserves. Mr. Packard says it just right and Webster's Unabridged Dictionary supports him.

"WRIGHT (rit), n. [ME wrighte, from AS. wyrhia, a worker, workman, maker, creator, from wyrcan, to work.] One who makes or constructs; a workman; as in shipwright, wheelwright, etc." The distance from playwrite to playwright is much more than the spelling of a word.

Truman Capote once made a sharp distinction between people who write and people who typewrite. We of the theatre, actors and directors alike, must constantly remind ourselves that we must make distinctions between writing for the page and writing for the stage.

Mr. Packard does more than this; he makes us remember what the Greek orators never forgot—that the key to eloquence is action, always action.

So, from Neil Simon's neat nifty that playwriting is not writing but rewriting, to George Kaufman's urging us to get "them X-ray eyes," or Walter Kerr's elbowing us to "see around corners," we now have Mr. William Packard's book, which is not about writing or playwrighting but about play creation. I welcome it.

Gene Frankel

Gene Frankel has left his mark on all areas of the American theatre —Broadway, off-Broadway, regional theatre and television. His major directing credits on Broadway include Indians *with Stacey Keach, and Maxwell Anderson's* Lost in the Stars. *A three time Obie winner, Mr. Frankel teaches his own theatre workshops.*

PROLOGUE

WHY WRITE PLAYS?

Imagine sitting in a theatre—the house lights are bright, there is an excited awareness in the air, then a sudden hush as the lights die down and there is darkness and silence before the front curtain begins to rise and the stage lights come up on the set. And for an instant it feels as if one is about to enter into a dream state where anything can take place, because this theatre is an arena that seems to be more real than one's own everyday world.

This is the beginning of magic in the theatre, where the stage becomes a sacred place and one approaches it with awe as one approaches anything that opens out onto the unknown. It is an art form that can take ordinary appearances and transform them into extraordinary realities, through the invisible craft of dramatic action. It is an experience of the illimitable possibilities of the shapes and faces of life, as Eugene O'Neill describes it:

> I mean the one true theatre, the age-old theatre, the theatre of the Greeks and the Elizabethans, a theatre that could dare to boast—without committing a farcical sacrilege—that it is a legitimate descendant of the first theatre that sprang, by virtue of man's imaginative interpretation of life, out of his worship of Dionysos. I mean a theatre returned to its highest and sole significant function as a Temple where the religion of a poetical interpretation of life is communicated to human beings, starved in spirit by their soul-stifling daily struggle to exist as masks among the masks of the living![1]

And throughout history, this one true theatre has existed wherever there have been true playwrights who were capable of imparting their own imaginative interpretation of life to the audiences who came to see their plays. For the Greek theatre of Epidaurus, it was Aeschylus and Sophocles; for the Globe Theatre in England, it was Shakespeare; for the Comédie-Française in Paris, it was Molière; for the Moscow Art Theatre in Russia, it was Chekhov; and for the Berliner Ensemble in Germany, it was Bertolt Brecht.

Unfortunately for us, in our modern commercial Broadway theatre, it is too often the producers and the directors and the star actors—to say nothing of the set designers and the choreographers and the lighting technicians, as well as their respective unions—who substitute for the playwright and his vital role in the theatrical process. Or in our regional theatres, too often it is the millions of dollars which are initially invested in a lot of fancy new theatre complexes which may then stand idle for long periods of time, or else are converted into swanky dinner-theatres where a desperate management throws together a few classy revivals of sure-fire old standards to make ends meet. We don't ever seem to have had the faith in the central place of the playwright in this country which is needed to create a truly contemporary American theatre.

The irony is that we do have the playwrights. Take any twelve outstanding contemporary dramatists you can think of: David Berry, Christopher Durang, John Guare, David Hare, Beth Henley, Israel Horovitz, Arthur Kopit, David Mamet, Marsha Norman, David Rabe, Sam Shepard, and Lanford Wilson—these playwrights have already created a body of work that is impressive in its own right, and which also goes a long way towards restoring the art of playwriting to its rightful place at the heart of the one true theatre.

This book is devoted to the exploration of dramatic techniques that can create magic in the theatre. It describes the practical craft of how plays are made, how to use actions and onstage visuals, and how to approach the appropriate development of character, dialogue, motifs, plots, and conflicts. The book is also intended for the theatre-lover and playgoer who wants to know more about the principles of dramatic action that playwrights have used through the ages. These dramatic principles are spelled out in any number of books of theory—in Aristotle's *Poetics*, in Nietzsche's *The Birth of Tragedy*, and in Artaud's *The Theatre and its Double*, and in Stanislavsky's *My Life in Art, An Actor Prepares, Building a Character*, and *Creating a Role*—but these dramatic principles are also to be found in all the great plays that have ever been written and performed in the great world theatres. What we have to do here is try to unite theory and practice, so we can give fresh expression and real relevance to the most important principles of dramatic action.

Incidentally, throughout the course of this book we will be using the masculine pronouns "he" and "his" to stand for the playwright, although this is simply for the sake of grammatical convenience. The theatre today is more open to women playwrights and readers and critics and actresses and audiences than at any time in its history —so when we say "his theatre," we are really saying "his or her theatre."

And one other thing: before we proceed to any discussion of the dynamics of dramatic principles in this book, we had better be very clear as to the motivation behind why people try to write plays in the first place. When there is so much more money to be made in writing almost anything other than plays—for example, novels or short stories or essays or biographies or straight journalism—why do so many playwrights persist in trying to write plays? We've all heard nightmare stories about how maddening it can be to take part in the chaotic collaborative work of the theatre, where so many mistakes can be made from first casting to final directorial interpretation, and where everyone from the actors to the stagehands may insist on having input on the writer's lines. And even if the playwright should manage to get his play produced in any reasonable facsimile of his original intention, that's no guarantee that an audience will receive it without being fickle or recalcitrant or plain cold.

So the question becomes very important for us to settle at the outset: why should any writer in his right mind keep returning to this particular art form of playwriting, when it's obviously not as lucrative or secure or soul-satisfying as any number of other outlets he could find for his writing?

To answer this question, we have to go back to the origins of drama as the earliest of all art forms. 50,000 years ago, before the first cave man evolved the most primitive spoken or pictorial communication, he had to signal his wants and fears and needs to his fellow cave men through a series of awkward mime gestures and crude dramatic visuals. As in our earliest infancy, the first human impulse has always been to show through pointing and gesturing, with our hands or with whatever other visuals may be immediately available to us. Thus *showing* comes before *telling*, and drama comes before language, and in this way primitive theatre began before the great epic narrative poems or histories or novels or short stories or essays. Drama is, quite simply, the most primitive form of human expression imaginable.

With time, drama grew into something much more than a simple signalling of human needs—in Greece, it developed into a ritual chant and dance and it also took on the drunken frenzy and the wild rhythmic movement we associate with certain contemporary rock stars. In fact the word "tragedy" comes from "tragoidia" or goat-song, and signifies the death and resurrection of Dionysos, the god of fertility and drunkenness. So the first Greek dance-drama Tragedies have all the primal passion of prayer and orgy, and they show the eternal conflict between the cool lucid Apollo logic of consciousness and the dark unconscious sexual poetry of Dionysos. Not that the Greek theatre was always so deadly serious—the Tragedies were invariably accompanied by satyr plays which were phallic romps and bawdy satirical farces which poked fun at the great mythic stories that had just taken place on stage. Even so, those soaring heroic plays like *Agamemnon* and *Oedipus Rex* and *The Trojan Women* depict the human psyche in its truest intuitive rhythms, and they are such exalted statements of our human condition that even today they can still evoke our deepest hopes and fears.

There were strong conventions that guided the development of this Greek drama. For example, during the performance of every tragedy there was always an altar to Dionysos onstage that was in full view of the audience, so there could be no overt violence performed in the course of the play. Thus Medea kills her children offstage, Clytemnestra murders Agamemnon behind the closed doors of the palace, and Oedipus tears out his eyes within the walls of his house—and these actions are then reported by messengers who come onstage to describe the violent events. There was also the chorus, which chanted and sang and danced throughout the play, and this gave the playwright an opportunity to create his own very special kind of dramatic language. And the Greek audiences were so attuned to the music of this language that they knew when a chorus went into a complicated verse form strophe, that it was going to be followed by another equally complicated verse form anti-strophe —and heaven help anyone in the chorus who missed a beat in the rhythm, because the audience would know it immediately and might just take that person offstage afterwards and punish him by giving him a good punch in the stomach.

Yet for all the greatness of this early Greek drama, and for all the overwhelming power of these magnificent Tragedies, even so, we can still sense there had always been a subtle distrust of the theatre, beginning with the first playwright, Thespis, around 560 B.C., who started spoken drama by standing on a table and shouting back at the chorus. Solon the law-giver did not approve of this because, as he said, Thespis sounded too much like "a theatrical liar." And over a hundred years later, Aristotle praised *Oedipus Rex* as the greatest play ever written, although we know that this Sophocles tragedy did not win first prize when it was performed in 425 B.C.—perhaps because the incest and parricide of the play was too much even for Athenian audiences. And as the years went on, this subtle distrust of the theatre grew more and more until it had become a very real persecution and prohibition against all drama. In the fourth century A.D., Augustine condemned the theatre as a thoroughly worthless and corrupt excess of his profligate youth:

> Stage-plays also carried me away, full of images of my miseries and of fuel to my fire. Why is it that man desires to be made sad beholding doleful and tragical things, which yet himself would by no means suffer? Yet he desires as a spectator to feel sorrow at them, and this very sorrow is his pleasure. What is this but a miserable madness?[2]

"A miserable madness"—Augustine was reacting to the cruel and crass and melodramatic Roman theatre which was presented in North Africa during the fourth century A.D. Nevertheless, Augustine's notion of theatre as "a miserable madness" lived on as an undercurrent attitude through the entire Middle Ages, when theatre as we know it was expressly forbidden by the Church and only craft guilds were allowed to put on carefully censored miracle and mystery plays which illustrated the medieval Catholicism of that era.

This historical bias against theatre continued into the Renaissance —Shakespeare himself had to write his plays under the watchful eye of the Master of the Revels who was appointed in 1581 to suppress profanity and other outrages in plays before they could be performed in public. Even so, Shakespeare was able to write plays of such vast and passionate scope that they encompassed the endless energy of life itself. Plays like *Romeo and Juliet, Julius Caesar, Hamlet, Othello, Macbeth, King Lear, Henry V, Twelfth Night, A Midsummer Night's Dream, The Merchant of Venice,* and *The Tempest* represent an explosion of language with a vocabulary of over 15,000 words, including words newly coined by Shakespeare, technical terms from the fields of music, astronomy, navigation, warfare, and the court, and street terms that were not usually heard in polite conversation.

But the real genius of Shakespeare lies not just in his mastery of language, magnificent as that language is—it is his use of extraordinarily strong and clear dramatic actions which are almost always embodied in the most remarkable onstage visuals. Shakespeare knew he had various stage levels and technical effects at his disposal in the Globe Theatre, and he shaped his plays accordingly. The Globe stage had balconies, inner and outer rooms, curtains to hide behind, trap doors, and a large forestage for direct address to the audience—so Shakespeare filled his plays with balcony scenes, eavesdropping scenes, plays within plays, sudden appearances and disappearances of ghosts and ghouls and gravediggers, and of course, dramatic soliloquys on the forestage. The result is the most comprehensive theatre that has ever been achieved, a miraculous fusion of language and actions and visuals, which is the height of the art of playwriting.

Yet for all the genius of Shakespeare, the repression of theatre kept right on during his own lifetime. In Elizabethan England the profession of playwriting was considered a second-rate trade, perhaps a few pegs above bear-baiting and witch-hunting—how else can we explain the virtual anonymity of Shakespeare himself, and the evident disregard of his achievement by practically all his compatriots and contemporaries? And outside his own country, the Kirk of Scotland was so outraged by these shocking new plays, that he tried to prohibit all theatrical productions of them, and when that proved unsuccessful, the Kirk forbade people from attending the performances. And a few years after the death of Shakespeare, at the time of the Puritan Revolution in 1642, the good men of God couldn't wait to close down the London theatres and end this pesky English drama as quickly as possible. For all the genius of William Shakespeare, the theatre was still considered, as Augustine had perceived it to be, nothing but "a miserable madness."

In our modern world, the subtle distrust of the theatre persists as a curious repression. Stanislavsky, the great Russian director and actor and co-founder of the Moscow Art Theatre, and the pioneer teacher of modern "method" acting theory, tells us an astonishing thing about himself in his autobiography:

> Often I was forced to play in the company of suspicious-looking people. What could I do? There were no other places to act, and I so wanted to act. Among these amateurs there were gamblers and demimondaines. And I, a man of position, a director of the Russian Musical Society, found that it was dangerous for my reputation if I appeared. It was necessary to hide behind some pseudonym. I sought a strange name, thinking that it would hide my early identity. I had known an amateur by the name of Doctor Stanislavsky. He had stopped playing, and I decided to adopt his name, thinking that behind a name as Polish as Stanislavsky no one could ever recognize me.[3]

Remarkable!—this father of modern acting technique felt so "embarrassed" by the theatrical profession, he felt he had to change his name to protect his family and his reputation from scandal! His real name was Konstantine Sergeyevich Aleyev, yet the name we know him by today—a name which is not at all Russian, but Polish—is his adopted name, "Stanislavsky." What better metaphor for theatre as a kind of "miserable madness," than that its greatest modern teacher and director felt he had to deceive people in order to participate in it!

Stanislavsky's changing his name may remind us of the modern practice of actors changing their names to work in the theatre or in films. During the days of the studio system in Hollywood, it was not unusual for producers to want to shape their actors so they would have absolute appeal for a mass audience, and that usually meant creating new names for them—especially if their given names seemed to be too ethnic or idiosyncratic or plain odd to suit the fancy of the studio personnel. Another reason for changing a name is that both professional unions—Actors Equity and the Screen Actors Guild—have strict rules prohibiting any member from using the

name of a previously established actor. This is for obvious professional reasons, to prevent one actor from drawing on the fame and
following of another actor—so the exclusive use of a name by one
actor is like copyrighting a commercial property. Some other actors
may have changed their names for the same reasons of "personal
embarrassment" that Stanislavsky cited. Or there may have been a
combination of reasons at work. In any event, here is a list of some
well known show business personalities, with their real names and
their professional names:

Isidore Itskowitz	Eddie Cantor
Arthur Jefferson	Stan Laurel
Douglas Ulman	Douglas Fairbanks
W. C. Dukinfield	W. C. Fields
Samuel Goldfish	Samuel Goldwyn
Gladys Smith	Mary Pickford
Sean O'Feeny	John Ford
Ehrich Weiss	Harry Houdini
Bernie Schwartz	Tony Curtis
Marion Morrison	John Wayne
Charles Edward Pratt	Boris Karloff
Richard Jenkins	Richard Burton
Norma Jean Baker	Marilyn Monroe
Frances Gumm	Judy Garland
Archie Leach	Cary Grant
Frank Cooper	Gary Cooper
Robert Zimmerman	Bob Dylan

To be sure, one can think of many other actors who did not change
their names upon entering show business—there are the older
veteran actors who may already have become known in their
original home countries, like Joseph Schildkraut, Vittorio Gassman,
Ricardo Montalban, Oscar Homolka, Omar Sharif, George Tobias,
and Peter Lorre—and there is also the younger generation of actors
who may not feel any strong ethnic or professional or personal
reasons for changing their names, like John Cassavetes, John Travol-
ta, Sylvester Stallone, Liza Minelli, Liv Ullman, Sissy Spacek, Robert
De Niro, and Maximilian Schell.

There are other examples of a subtle distrust of the theatre in our
daily lives. We talk about someone "acting out" his problems, or we
tell our children to "stop showing off," or we remember that in our
own childhood we were told not to be "so theatrical"—all of these
things being very casual put-downs of an honorable profession. We

don't go around telling people to "stop being so medical," or cautioning children not to be "so legal," and we don't recall ever being told in our own childhood not to be "so editorial." Worst of all, if our sons or daughters should ever say they want to go into the theatre, we feel there must be something radically cuckoo about such a choice—we may tell them it's okay to give it a go, but secretly we hope they'll outgrow all this silliness and eventually opt for a sensible job like designing new cars or being a transit cop or selling life insurance.

How can we account for this subtle distrust of the theatre that is all around us? We could say there has always been a strong Western taboo against our ever revealing our deepest feelings to anyone, because we are living in a culture that is so hellbent on the concealment of truth on every level. But the reason must go even deeper than that. The German poet Rilke may have gotten close to it in *The Notebooks of Malte Laurids Brigge*, when he wrote:

> Let us be honest about it, then; we have no theatre, any more than we have a God: for this, community is needed.[4]

That is, the subtle distrust of the theatre may not be merely a failure of our culture, it may be the failure of our civilization and religion to keep up with the monstrous moral and psychic and religious crises of our time—the worship of technology for its own sake, the global population explosion, and the possibility of our own nuclear annihilation.

The Swedish playwright August Strindberg came to the same conclusion as Rilke did, that theatre and religion were the two major casualties of modern civilization, when he said:

> Theatre, like religion, is on the way to being discarded as a dying form . . .[5]

And Antonin Artaud, in *The Theatre and its Double*, saw theatre as the last chance for us to shake loose from all of our lives' lies and "make our demons flow":

> We cannot go on prostituting the idea of theatre whose only value is in its excruciating, magical relation to reality and danger.[6]

If this is so—if theatre in our time has suffered the destitution and estrangement and senselessness of our era—then we would expect our playwrights to feel this failure most keenly in their own lives. And in fact we find the contemporary playwright is usually the least appreciated and the most tampered-with artisan in a hopelessly archaic industry. We remember with great shame and sadness how Tennessee Williams was so mercilessly badgered during the last fifteen years of his life, to keep proving that he had not "lost his talent"—as if any major artist ever had to prove anything to anyone. And we can understand why Arthur Miller says he was tempted many times to "swear off" the art of playwriting altogether:

> Had there been a working theatre, it could have been or might have been otherwise. After all, I haven't had a continuing relationship with a critic—except with Harold Clurman in a way. We have no real theatre. We have shows, which isn't really the same thing.[7]

Yet for all the subtle distrust of the theatre, we also realize that we are in the midst of an extraordinary period of contemporary playwriting. We already listed twelve American playwrights earlier in this chapter—we could just as easily go on and list another twelve: Ed Bullins, Jack Gelber, James Leo Herlihy, Hugh Leonard, William Mastrosimone, Mark Medoff, Leonard Melfi, John Ford Noonan, John Pielmeir, Miguel Pinero, Murray Shisgal, and Wendy Wasserstein. We will be dealing with all of these playwrights, and more, in a later chapter of this book. The point is that these writers are continuing to create an ongoing theatre that is more open and daring than any theatre since the Renaissance. We just don't have a contemporary American theatre to keep encouraging and developing their work, and the work of dozens of others.

To be sure, we're talking here about a theatre that is significant and enduring and relevant to our era. We realize there will always be a place in our culture for another sort of theatre, a theatre of "entertainment"—and let's not fool ourselves, it takes as much mastery of the basic dramatic principles to create excellent musical comedies such as *South Pacific* or *Kiss Me, Kate* or *My Fair Lady,* or good Neil Simon comedies like *The Odd Couple* or *The Goodbye Girl* or *The Prisoner of Second Avenue,* as it does to write an experimental play such as Eugene O'Neill's *Strange Interlude* or Edward Albee's *Tiny Alice.*

But as we said at the outset, one had better be very clear as to the motivation behind one's effort to write plays in the first place. Is it for entertainment? Fame? Wealth? To show off one's talents? These are pretty tacky and opportunistic reasons for doing anything, although god knows in this world they're probably as valid as any other reasons, so long as one is honest about them. There are plenty of playwrights turning out competent scripts for Broadway and off-Broadway and off-off-Broadway, and for regional theatres, and most of all for television, who are mostly motivated by the need for a weekly paycheck, and who have no higher aspiration than meeting a particular deadline. These playwrights have sufficient command of the basic dramatic principles so they can manufacture lots of facile plots and stock characters and cardboard situations, and sometimes they can even come up with effective vehicles for *tour de force* acting performances. The vast quantity of drama scripts for American television is created by playwrights of this calibre, and we should at least have the decency to pay tribute to their professionalism. Someone has to turn out all that stuff, and not everyone could function well under such pressured circumstances, so after all they are performing a necessary service to the community.

But there are other playwrights who would quite simply go out of their minds if they were expected to come up with adequate scripts for the hybrid and synthetic monolith of television and the commercial theatre. Under the anxiety and pressure of cranking out patchwork and formula plays for an unseen and an unseeing audience, these playwrights would lose all sense of who they were and why they were trying to write, and that would render them incapable of going on.

Chekhov said this best in a letter to a friend:

> There are moments when I completely lose heart. For whom and for what do I write? For the public? But I don't see it, and believe in it less than I do in spooks; it is uneducated, badly brought up, and its best elements are unfair and insincere to us. Write for the sake of money? But I never have any money and not being used to it I am indifferent to it . . . Write for the sake of praise? But praise merely irritates me . . .

Chekhov goes on to give his own reason for writing plays:

> My holy of holies is the human body, health, intelligence, talent, inspiration, love, and the most resolute freedom—freedom from violence and lying, whatever forms they may take. That is the program I would follow if I were a great artist.[8]

And Tennessee Williams once said something similar about why he wrote plays:

Define it as the passion to create, which is all we know of God.

In other words, one creates dramatic actions and onstage visuals because this is quite simply the deepest instinct that we know, and because it is also our strongest response to life itself. And if this act of creation has to take place in a theatre which some people see as "a miserable madness," why then, miserable it certainly is, and madness it may well be, but still it is the clearest mirror that we have for who we are and why we are as we are.

One last word, about theatre audiences. For us to have any authentic contemporary American theatre, it's not enough to have important playscripts and significant productions and outstanding performances. We also have to have audiences that are alive and responsive to the full implications of the playwright's art; otherwise there can be no real growth or continuity from one show to the next show. And we've seen too many examples of outstanding regional theatres failing or falling out of favor, simply because they could not sustain the commitment of a dedicated audience for the introduction of new works by promising young playwrights. And the question is always in the air—what is the secret of attracting and keeping vitally alive theatre audiences?

We don't have any answers for how truly great theatre audiences come about or how they can be nurtured and sustained, but we can describe what the best theatre audiences are like. Here are some examples:

1. In Athens, an audience would spend a full day at the theatre, arrive at sun-up, see three full-length major plays with one or two satyr plays in between, and then the audience would break to eat over the afternoon, until it was time to go back and see one last full-length comedy at the end of the day. These Greek audiences thought nothing of spending from six to nine hours a day at the theatre.

2. In the Elizabethan theatre, an audience would play cards, drink ale, pick up women, toss orange peels, make catcalls, and crack nuts. This audience would be composed of raucous groundlings, lords in boxes, and an occasional patron sitting right on the stage itself. And while this description may make that Elizabethan audience out to be completely unmanageable, Shakespeare knew this was just the audience to appreciate and understand a play such as *Hamlet* or *King Lear*.

3. In the modern theatre, on February 25, 1830, when Victor Hugo's play *Hernani* was produced at the Comèdie-Française, the text broke all the conventions of the classical alexandrine line—there were no caesu-

ras, so the sense of a sentence went spilling over from one line to the next. Unforgiveable!—the audience booed and hooted this insult to the neoclassic French theatre. But there were others in the audience who were delighted to hear a modern poetry that was finally freed from the strictures of Racine and Corneille, and men such as Gautier and Balzac and Delacroix and Berlioz rose to cheer the new play. And this audience was booing and cheering not for *what* was being said, but for *how* it was being said!

4. In 1971, David Rabe won an Obie Award for *The Basic Training of Pavel Hummel,* presented by Joseph Papp at the Public Theatre in New York, and in 1972 Rabe received a Tony Award for *Sticks and Bones.* Both plays were searing indictments of the effects of the Vietnam war on America and Americans, and both were produced in America while that war was still active in the minds and lives of the theatre audiences. Yet the audience was willing to support these indictments, even see one of them, *Sticks and Bones,* moved uptown to the commercial Broadway theatre. Rabe speaks of his feelings about this relocation of his play:

> My idea was that perhaps the future of serious theatre in New York depended on abandoning Broadway. Let Broadway become the circus it seemed to want to be. Get all the playwrights, even the most prestigious, to think off-Broadway as the place for their work. We were being deluded by our outdated legend about the glamour of Broadway. Good writer after good writer, it seemed, had been foundering on the rocks uptown. Perhaps Broadway was no longer the place where good writing was tested against the best work of others, both current and time-honored.[9]

5. In 1980, Christopher Durang received an Obie Award for *Sister Mary Ignatius Explains it All For You,* which is an acid satire on the Catholic Church and its traditional catechism and practices, and it is also an iconoclastic attack on how the Church produces spiritual castrati who are incapable of perceiving the realities of the modern world. Daring and audacious and hilarious, and able to stun audiences with its outrageous humor, nonetheless this play received the highest off-Broadway award.

These examples of how great audiences can help to nurture great theatre, may offer us some promise for the future. Because throughout history, these two elements have always been inextricably linked—audiences and playwrights, playwrights and audiences.

This book tries to speak to both the serious playwright and the serious playgoer, in order to introduce both of them to the basic dramatic principles and techniques which make for the magic of the one true theatre.

CHAPTER 1

DRAMATIC VERSUS NARRATIVE

The most important thing for a playwright to realize about playwriting is that there is a crucial difference between dramatic and narrative writing.

Aristotle in the *Poetics* says all plays must be written "in a dramatic, not in a narrative form"—but what is the difference between these two kinds of writing? We know a novel is not a play, and we know the skills and abilities that go into shaping a good narrative story are not necessarily the same skills and abilities that go into shaping a good dramatic play. But we need to get very clear right away about these two different approaches to writing the same subject matter.

Dramatic and narrative—how can we illustrate the difference between these two forms? Here is an example that may show us the difference: there are two radically different treatments of the same situation—one of them is narrative and the other is dramatic:

1. A drunk is sitting in a bar and he starts telling the audience the story of his life. He tells anecdote after anecdote about how he has been misunderstood and frustrated by everyone he has ever known. The stories are all amusing and well told and they all illustrate the same point, which is why this poor man has ended up as the hopeless drunk that he is today.

2. The same drunk is in the same bar and he does not say one single word, he just takes a bottle and sends it smashing up against the wall.

It's surprising how many people would say that the first version is the better treatment of the situation—perhaps because it has all those well told stories which make for good background exposition and character development. And that is probably so from a narrative point of view, because the first version is literary and descriptive and would probably read better on the page.

But the second version is really the more appropriate dramatic treatment of the situation, because it has a strong dramatic action and embodies that action in a vivid onstage visual. One would have to imagine the bottle being smashed up against the wall, to realize what a powerfully effective happening it would be onstage—it would say all that really needs to be said about the utter hopelessness of this drunk, and it would say it without using any words at all.

Of course we've deliberately overstated our case and we've used an example that may seem too simplistic, but that's because we want to make our point as strongly and as clearly as possible—that one good onstage visual which embodies a dramatic action is worth a thousand words.

That's not to say it wouldn't also be important to have some helpful narrative elements in that scene, to complement the strong action and the visual of throwing the bottle up against the wall. We might want to use a few of those narrative anecdotes that the drunk tells about his past life, and perhaps we might let him have an imaginary dialogue with one or two of his dead drunk friends, to show more of his strong character action.

But our basic point remains—for a scene to be truly dramatic, it must derive its central power from a strong major action and a vivid onstage visual.

Dramatic and narrative—this may seem to be a subtle distinction, but it's far-reaching in its implications, and unless one can master this crucial difference between dramatic and narrative writing, one can't hope to write a very good play.

We can summarize the difference between dramatic and narrative writing in this way:

NARRATIVE. The genius of narrative writing is in the *telling* of a story that has a beginning and a middle and an end, and there is usually a narrator who leads the reader step by step through the story line. And the narrative will invariably include a good deal of background material and specific detail description to help develop the exposition of setting and plot and character.

DRAMATIC. In dramatic writing, instead of telling a story, one *shows* it—through strong dramatic actions that are embodied in powerful onstage visuals. And in drama, one does not always begin at the beginning, one usually plunges the audience right into the middle of an action so there will not be so much need for all that introductory background material. Of course there will have to be *some* narrative elements in any good drama—some skillful exposition is always essential so one can develop the "given circumstances" of the scene, and there will also be a need for sharp dialogue to show the interaction of the characters. But the important thing is always what is happening right there onstage—which is to say, the actions and the visuals.

Or to boil the whole thing down to the simplest terms possible, the most important thing about dramatic writing is:

DON'T TELL US—SHOW US.

Now for some reason this is a very difficult point to get across to most people, perhaps because most people have been so thoroughly conditioned in the non-visual, verbal, narrative tradition. It's a good deal more pervasive than most people realize, because they probably went to schools where they had to read a lot of narrative novels, short stories, histories, and biographies—and then they probably had to write a lot of narrative term paper reports about all these narrative works. And these same people still read narrative stories in newspapers and magazines, and they also listen to narrative play-by-play descriptions of football and baseball and hockey games on the radio and television, and then they watch anchormen come on and deliver the narrative evening news on TV. In fact, most people have been surrounded by so much narrative writing and thinking and feeling all of their lives that they assume narrative is the only really valid form of expression. So when these people go to the theatre to see a new play, they may be open enough to a powerful dramatic experience, but even so, they usually can't wait to get home and read narrative reviews of the play in the newspapers the next day. It's not that these people don't trust their own judgment about the play; it's just that their unconscious need for narrative is so strong that they feel curiously incomplete until any dramatic experience has been safely translated into linear narrative terms. And if something should ever happen to these people on the street, they can't wait to get on the phone and tell someone else all about it—which reveals the same instinct for translating dramatic action back into narrative form.

It's as if most people secretly believe that narrative writing and thinking and feeling somehow have more legitimacy than dramatic writing and thinking and feeling.

We can see the absurdity of this attitude every time an eccentric scholar comes scuttling out of the woodwork to declare that Francis Bacon or the Earl of Oxford or some other English lord wrote all those plays of Shakespeare, because Bacon and Oxford and the other lord were educated and aristocratic gentlemen who were masters of narrative writing, and therefore they were much more capable of writing the plays than poor William Shakespeare who was only a lowly actor and had merely mastered the second-rate art of dramatic writing. But behind this argument is the pernicious assumption that there is something inherently nobler and more exalted about narrative writing, which sets it far above the slightly sordid and less acceptable art of dramatic writing—which of course is nothing but a lot of pretentious nonsense.

Yet this peculiar confusion about narrative and dramatic writing persists to the present day, and it causes a great deal of very real chaos in the world of contemporary filmmaking. Certain movie producers have always taken narrative masterworks and tried to adapt them to dramatic form, and they can never quite figure out why certain great novels like Melville's *Moby Dick* or Mark Twain's *Huckleberry Finn* or Kurt Vonnegut Jr.'s *Slaughterhouse Five* will never quite translate completely into dramatic terms. Some of the film adaptations of these novels may be competent enough in their own way, but they can never hope to match the power and originality of the books on which they are based. *Moby Dick* was first made as a silent film, *The Sea Beast,* and then in 1930 it was a far-fetched film with John Barrymore and Joan Bennett that tried to evoke our pity for the brave one-legged Ahab after he had returned to shore; and then there was the disastrous 1956 Warner remake by John Huston and Ray Bradbury starring Gregory Peck, Richard Basehart, and Orson Welles, which was a lumbering and mechanical whale of a movie that *Variety* called "Interesting more often than exciting." *Huckleberry Finn* went through no less than four major film treatments—there was the 1931 Paramount early sound movie starring Jackie Coogan, the fairly good 1939 MGM movie starring Mickey Rooney, the makeshift 1960 MGM remake starring Archie Moore, Buster Keaton, Andy Devine, and Neville Brand, and then the 1974 United Artists musical version starring David Wayne and Gary Merrill, about which Tom Milne wrote, "It expires in a morass of treacle" and the *Illustrated London News* said, "It transforms a great work of fiction into something bland, boring, and tasteless." *Slaughterhouse Five* was Kurt Vonnegut Jr.'s attempt to make sense out of the utterly meaningless air raid firebombing of Dresden in World War II which claimed over 130,000 lives, and it was made into a 1972 Universal film about how Billy Pilgrim, a shy optometrist, keeps zigzagging across time and space from a Nazi prisoner-of-war camp to the idyllic planet of Tralfamadore—and though this film version was interesting enough, starring Michael Sacks and Ron Liebman and the music of Johann Sebastian Bach, film critic Stanley Kauffmann wrote, "A lot of good makings in this picture; but very little is made."

As we said, these films may all be very competent in the way they capture the simplest story line of the narrative novels they are based on, but none of them are able to translate the unique narrative genius of Melville or Mark Twain or Vonnegut into compelling dramatic terms. And after all, the narrative genius is what makes *Moby Dick* and *Huckleberry Finn* and *Slaughterhouse Five* into the irresistible masterpieces that they are.

The same thing happens with short story and novella masterpieces, like Poe's *The Pit and the Pendulum* and D. H. Lawrence's *The Fox* and Ernest Hemingway's *The Snows of Kilimanjaro*—they also tend to fall flat when they are translated into dramatic terms. *The Pit and the Pendulum* is one of Poe's great works with a powerful subtext of incest and satanism, but the 1961 film with Vincent Price is just a lugubriously gruesome Gothic saga of how a brother tosses two lovers into a torture den, and the film is punctuated by all sorts of loud thunderclaps and bright lightning bolts and a lot of silly still shots of ancient castles. Lawrence's novella *The Fox* is about two girls,

Branford and March, who become obsessed by a fox which is stealing fowls on their isolated place, and this fox becomes a subtle image of some mysterious sexual force that will have its dark way with the girls—but in the 1967 Warner film starring Anne Heywood and Sandy Dennis, all the subtlety is lost and the movie becomes, as Leslie Halliwell comments, "Rather obvious sexual high jinks full of symbolism and heavy breathing." And *The Snows of Kilimanjaro,* Hemingway's short story masterpiece about a white hunter in Africa who is dying of gangrene and is beset by hyenas and his own bad memories, was made into an absolutely awful 1952 Darryl F. Zanuck film starring Gregory Peck and Susan Hayward and Ava Gardner —and as *Newsweek* Magazine wrote, "The succinct and vivid qualities associated with Hemingway are rarely evoked, and what has been substituted is for the most part meandering, pretentious and more or less maudlin romance."

Now most people who went to see any of these films may have liked them well enough as films, although they probably went home saying to themselves, "Well I guess it was okay, but somehow I liked the book much better." And these people wouldn't have the slightest clue as to why these films had subtly failed, because these people wouldn't be able to sense the underlying basic problem of what is so damnably difficult about trying to translate narrative into dramatic form.

What is this underlying basic problem? Why is it virtually impossible to adapt a great narrative work into dramatic form, without an overwhelming sense of loss and omission? Could it be that we're dealing here with two completely separate mediums, like oil painting and sculpture, which may have very strong similarities but are clearly so radically different in their basic nature that they have their own separate and distinct principles and processes?

It's beginning to look that way, and yet if that is indeed the case, we need to make ourselves aware of what these different principles and processes are all about. Let's look at a very specific example that will show the radical difference between narrative and dramatic writing. Here are the opening lines of a great narrative novel:

It is a little remarkable, that—though disinclined to talk overmuch of myself and my affairs at the fireside, and to my personal friends—an autobiographical impulse should twice in my life have taken possession of me, in addressing the public.[1]

This is the beginning of *The Scarlet Letter* by Nathaniel Hawthorne. We are being presented here with a casual prose narrator who is leisurely and reflective, someone who tells us he has a certain timidity about delving into the awful psychological story that is about to unfold in the harsh, stark, relentlessly judgmental world of New England Puritanism. And this narrator is about to tell us a story of how the mother of an illegitimate child has to wear a scarlet letter for adultery, because she will not reveal that the father of the child is the village minister. Now this may strike us as a peculiarly cruel and painful story, but that is precisely why this narrator's gentle and reassuring voice is there to lead us into the oppressive mood and gloom of the background atmosphere and setting and story of *The Scarlet Letter.*

But at this point we may be wondering, how could anyone ever put this narrator's voice onstage, or use it in any film version of the novel? One couldn't just have the narrator saying these lines on the side of the stage, or reciting them as voice-over on the sound track of a film, because that would only create a major distraction from the story line and it would make the adaptation so literary and talky that the greatest actors in the world couldn't possibly fake their way through and make the film dramatic. As the film critic James Agee wrote in a review for *The Nation* of Albert Lewin's version of Oscar Wilde's *The Picture of Dorian Gray,* "I wish somebody would take book lovers like Mr. Lewin aside and explain to them, once for all, that to read from the text of a novel—not to mention interior monologues —when people are performing on the screen, while it may elevate the literary tone of the production, which I doubt, certainly and inescapably plays hell with it as a movie."[2] No, one cannot hold onto the narrative as narrative, if one is trying to make a dramatic adaptation of a story or a novel—one has to find a way of translating that narrative into an equivalent dramatic action, and that will not always be an easy job. Indeed, in some cases it may not even be possible.

And in fact it's not at all possible further on in *The Scarlet Letter,* because that central image of the scarlet letter "A" which Hester Prynne has been forced to wear on the outside of her clothing has become so narrative in character, and it depends so much on how it is being *told* to us, that if we tried to *show* it onstage or in filmic terms, we would be robbing it of all its true power and magical ambiguity. And at the end of the novel, Reverend Dimmesdale is standing on the town scaffold in front of his congregation, when he suddenly rips open his shirt. Is there a scarlet letter "A" there on his own chest, and does it really give off an eerie psychological glow? The reader can't be sure, and Hawthorne himself writes the narrative so carefully that the scene remains unclear. Here is the description of that event in the novel:

> Most of the spectators testified to having seen, on the breast of the unhappy minister, a SCARLET LETTER—the very semblance of that worn by Hester Prynne—imprinted on his flesh . . .

But the narrative goes right on to say:

> . . . certain persons, who were spectators of the whole scene, and professed never once to have removed their eyes from the Reverend Mr. Dimmesdale, denied that there was any mark whatever on his breast, more than on a ncw-born infant's . . .[3]

In other words, that mysterious scarlet letter "A" existed on Dimmesdale's chest for some observers, but other observers thought there was no such thing. Perhaps Hawthorne wanted the reader to believe that this emblem of guilt existed only for those who chose to see it, or whose own lives had predisposed them to imagine such a thing in the hearts of other people. In any event, this entire scaffold scene is left deliberately vague and ambiguous, so the reader's mind will be haunted by the event long after he has finished reading it.

But how on earth could we ever begin to put such a thing onstage, or into a film version of the novel? We couldn't "show" something which half the audience could see and the other half couldn't see, unless we set up the seating arrangement of a theatre so the left hand side would get one version of the story and the right hand side would get another version—which would be absurd. Or unless we made the mistake of simply taking one point of view as the exclusively true one, and throwing away the other point of view altogether—which would be foolish.

However, Hollywood being the persistently absurd and foolish paradise that it is, that's exactly what did happen in the various film versions of *The Scarlet Letter*. Incredibly enough, there have been ten different cinematic adaptations of *The Scarlet Letter* to date: in the United States there were films in 1910, 1911, 1913, 1917, 1920, 1926, and 1934, a recent television version in 1979; a British version in 1922, and a German version in 1971. By far the most notable of these films was the 1926 MGM movie directed by Victor Sjostrom and starring Lillian Gish and Lars Hanson. And in that final scaffold scene we've been discussing, the unhappy minister is standing in front of his congregation and he suddenly rips open his shirt to reveal—a large scarlet letter "A"! And everyone down on the ground gasps and recoils in horror, faces turn away, hands cover over eyes, etc. It's a fairly effective dramatic moment in the film, although of course it has absolutely nothing whatsoever to do with Hawthorne's original narrative—we just saw how hard the author worked to leave this scene deliberately vague and ambiguous in the reader's mind, and here it has been changed into something quite arbitrary and theatrical. One almost feels as if the central point of the entire novel has been lost.

But as we said, one can't expect to be able to translate narrative into dramatic form, without an overwhelming sense of loss and omission. And it's a curse that works both ways, because it's just as impossible to translate a great dramatic work over into narrative terms, without there being just as much distortion and serious misunderstanding.

For example, here are the opening lines of a great dramatic play. The first thing we'll notice is that there is no leisurely and reflective narrator whose gentle and reassuring voice is there to lead us into the background atmosphere and setting and story line of the play—there are only the following brief stage directions:

Elsinore   *A platform before the castle. FRANCISCO at his post; Enter to him BARNARDO.*

Of course this is the beginning of *Hamlet* by William Shakespeare, and it is a great deal different from the opening of *The Scarlet Letter* by Hawthorne. Shakespeare tells us nothing of the oppressive mood and gloom of the harsh, stark world of medieval Denmark in these opening lines, nor does he pretend that he has any timidity about delving into the awful psychological story that is about to unfold about a young man who has to revenge the murder of his father. In fact, Shakespeare does not even bother telling us who Francisco and Bernardo are—he just plunges us right into their opening dialogue, with these lines:

BARNARDO: Who's there?
FRANCISCO: Nay, answer me: stand, and unfold yourself.

BARNARDO:	Long live the King!
FRANCISCO:	Barnardo?
BARNARDO:	He.
FRANCISCO:	You come most carefully upon your hour.
BARNARDO:	'Tis now struck twelve; get thee to bed, Francisco.
FRANCISCO:	For this relief much thanks; 'tis bitter cold,
	And I am sick at heart.
BARNARDO:	Have you had quiet guard?
FRANCISCO:	Not a mouse stirring.
BARNARDO:	Well, good night.
	If you do meet Horatio and Marcellus,
	The rivals of my watch, bid them make haste.
FRANCISCO:	I think I hear them. Stand ho! Who is there . . .⁴

There are very few lines here, yet a great deal of dramatic action is already happening—two guards confront each other in panic, they mix up their signals and shout out at each other, then they switch to being overly friendly as they broach the business of this evening's watch, they gingerly exchange the news that nothing has happened so far, they drop the subject, then there is quick panic again as they hear someone else approaching. Obviously both guards are on edge about something, yet they are not able to bring themselves to name what that something is. And all this takes place in only fourteen lines!

We can go further, and try to imagine what the onstage visuals will look like in this brief opening scene. The two guards are in full armor and they have weapons which they will aim at each other in the first few lines, then they will lower these weapons, then at the end of the lines they will raise their weapons again, this time towards something or someone that is approaching from offstage. These onstage visuals will be so powerful in this scene that even if we did not hear one single word of the dialogue, we would still be able to get a sense of what was happening, simply by looking at the way these guards are raising and lowering their weapons.

This is the height of dramatic writing—before we know what is happening, we are hurtled headlong into an action, and this action is embodied in bold clear visuals. And this isn't only in the plays of Shakespeare—we can look at another example of dramatic writing from the modern theatre and we will see the same strong actions and bold visuals, in part of a scene from Harold Pinter's play *The Homecoming*. Lenny is left alone onstage with his brother's wife Ruth, and Lenny begins talking to her. The action of the scene is very strong—Lenny is "checking her out," trying to determine how far he can push or poke or press or pinch or ultimately manipulate this woman for his own purposes. And he begins doing this by playing games with two seemingly insignificant physical objects, the ashtray and a glass of water:

LENNY: . . . Excuse me, shall I take this ashtray out of your way?
RUTH: It's not in my way.
LENNY: It seems to be in the way of your glass. The glass was about to fall. Or the ashtray. I'm rather worried about the carpet. It's not me, it's my father. He's obsessed with order and clarity. He doesn't like mess. So, as I don't believe you're smoking at the moment, I'm sure you won't object if I move the ashtray.

He does so.

And now perhaps I'll relieve you of your glass.
RUTH: I haven't quite finished.
LENNY: You've consumed quite enough, in my opinion.
RUTH: No, I haven't.
LENNY: Quite sufficient, in my own opinion.
RUTH: Not in mine, Leonard.

Pause.

LENNY: Don't call me that, please.
RUTH: Why not?
LENNY: That's the name my mother gave me.

Pause.

Just give me the glass.
RUTH: No.

Pause.

LENNY: I'll take it, then.
RUTH: If you take the glass . . . I'll take you.[5]

Halfway through this scene, there is a reversal of the major action: Ruth addresses Lenny by his given name, "Leonard," which stops him in his tracks. She then indicates that she will not allow him to continue playing games with those two seemingly insignificant physical objects, the ashtray and the glass of water—and that signals the audience that from this point on, the action of the play will be in Ruth's hands. And this has all been achieved without any narrative writing, because everything has been done through strong dramatic actions and the use of onstage visuals.

In these two short scenes from *Hamlet* and *The Homecoming,* a great deal is taking place in a very few lines, and obviously one could not translate these dramatic works into narrative form without a good deal of overwriting and explanation to convey all the things that are happening in the scenes—and even then one would not be able to communicate everything that would be taking place onstage. It's as if dramatic actions and onstage visuals open us out onto another dimension of reality, which narrative writing can only hint at; a good playscript is like a musical score that simply suggests how all these actions and visuals should be played.

Now we can summarize some of the crucial differences we've discovered between narrative and dramatic writing:

1. Narrative writing *tells* us something, whereas dramatic writing *shows* us something.

2. Narrative writing tends to be lengthy and expository, whereas dramatic writing tends to be brief and visual.

3. Narrative writing usually uses the voice of a narrator to lead us into the background atmosphere and setting and story line, whereas dramatic writing does not need a narrator because we see with our own eyes what is happening right there onstage. To be sure, there are some plays that do use "narrators", such as *Henry V* or *Our Town* or *A Glass Menagerie* or *Under Milkwood* or *A Man For All Seasons,* but this will invariably be to achieve some special effect by distancing us from the unique nature of the subject matter, or to bridge the unities of time and place and action in some extraordinary and experimental way.

4. Narrative writing almost always tells us about something that has already happened in the past tense, whereas dramatic writing always shows us something that is happening right now in front of us in the existential present.

In other words: narrative writing tells a story in somewhat lengthy and expository terms, usually using a narrator, and taking place sometime in the past—whereas dramatic writing shows a story in relatively brief visual scenes, does not usually use a narrator, and takes place in the here and now.

Narrative and dramatic writing—who knows why someone gravitates towards one form instead of the other? It may be a matter of individual taste or temperament or personal preference, or else it may be the peculiar circumstances of the age one lives in, or else it may be the instinctive God-given gift of genius that one is born with.

Whatever the reason, some authors are attracted to the pure challenge of narrative writing, or creating a distinctive and idiosyncratic style and texture of expression in prose narrative—authors such as Fyodor Dostoyevski, Franz Kafka, Thomas Mann, Marcel Proust, Charles Dickens, James Joyce, and William Faulkner. And other authors are attracted to the pure challenge of creating powerfully immediate dramatic actions and vivid onstage visuals—authors such as Aeschylus, William Shakespeare, Molière, Henrik Ibsen, George Bernard Shaw, Eugene O'Neill, and Tennessee Williams. How many writers can one think of, who have been able to excel in *both* narrative and dramatic forms of writing? In all history the list is not very long. Leo Tolstoy, Anton Chekhov, Victor Hugo, Oscar Wilde, Albert Camus, Thornton Wilder, Samuel Beckett—give or take a few names, that's about it. But this only reinforces our point, that the two forms of writing are radically different from one another, because their underlying principles and processes are so separate and distinct.

Even so, there are a great many people who may have some background and experience with narrative writing, and these people think they can wander into a theatre and write a play without having any previous training or experience in the basic principles of dramatic writing. This shows a maddening arrogance and disregard for the crucial difference between the two forms of writing, and it probably accounts for why there are so many unplayable playscripts that are scattered across the countryside. Because it's not just a matter of how much talent or intelligence or determination one may have—the truth is one has to develop an instinct for dramatic action and onstage visuals through continual practice, practice, practice of the craft. It's no accident that so many of our greatest playwrights, from Sophocles and Shakespeare and Molière to Harold Pinter and Sam Shepard and Christopher Durang, have all had extensive training as actors, because actors know what dramatic actions are and how these actions are expressed in onstage visuals. So perhaps the best way for a beginning playwright to get close to the basic principles of dramatic writing is to go out and act in a play, or else audit a good acting class and watch the way trained actors think and feel and behave.

These basic principles of dramatic action can be summed up in three words: *actions, visuals,* and *stakes.* And here is how these principles are applied to the art of playwriting:

1. *Drama is action.* Action is someone's wanting something. Action is the strong objective that someone has in a beat or scene or act of a play.

2. *Character is action.* Character is someone's wanting something. Character is his or her major objective in the play.

3. *Actions and characters should both be expressed through vivid onstage visuals.* A visual is any physical object that becomes the embodiment of some major action.

4. *Actions and characters run into obstacles.* Dramatic conflict begins when someone wants something but there is an obstacle (a strong resistance, a stone wall impediment, or some other character's action) that gets in the way of what this character wants. Then the character will either have to overcome the obstacle, or else the character will not be able to overcome the obstacle and so he will have to try and approach it from some other direction.

5. *The greatness of any action depends on how much is at stake.* The greater these stakes, the greater the action will be—and the smaller the stakes, the smaller the action will be. If the stakes aren't all that much, then a character won't care very much about his action, and then the audience won't care either.

Actions and visuals and stakes—these are the basic principles of dramatic writing. Obstacles figure as the beginning of plot and conflict in a play.

This may all seem easy enough at first glance, but like any technique of course it has to be mastered in practice. It's a little like learning how to throw a curve ball—you can study all sorts of charts and diagrams on how to do it, but unless you actually go out there on the mound and begin practicing the pitch, it's nothing but a lot of words on the page. But then the more you keep at it in actual practice, the closer you come to a gut hunch understanding of what it's all about, until sooner or later there will be a click inside your head and it has suddenly become second nature, part of your deepest instincts, and you don't have to "think" about it anymore. But it does take continual practice to get to this point.

So let's put these dramatic principles to work right away, and see how they apply to our earlier example of *Hamlet:*

1. *Drama is action.* The major action is Hamlet's wanting to avenge his murdered father. This is his action, and so it is his objective in the play, it is what he wants, and this action is behind everything that Hamlet says and does in the entire play. Incidentally, this same action of avenging a murdered father happens to be the action of three other characters in the

play—Ophelia, Laertes, and Fortinbras—so these will be subplot actions that will parallel the major action of Hamlet in the play. This overwhelmingly strong action destroys Ophelia's mind, and drives Laertes into a fatal duel with Hamlet. Only Fortinbras is able to execute his major action with a clear mind and military dispatch.

2. *Character is action.* Hamlet's dramatic character does not have anything to do with his being a prince or a Dane or a student at Wittenberg University, or his being moody or philosophical or the sort of person who likes to deliver a lot of poetic soliloquys. These things are all secondary to Hamlet's dramatic character or major action, which is his objective: to avenge his murdered father.

3. *Actions and characters are both expressed through vivid onstage visuals.* Hamlet's major action of wanting to avenge his murdered father is expressed visually throughout the play, from the opening scenes when we see him dressed in mourning for his father, through his putting on a play within a play to re-enact the murder of his father, to his final duel with Laertes who is using a poisoned foil. Hamlet finally kills Claudius and thereby completes his major action of avenging his murdered father.

4. *Actions and characters run into obstacles.* There are strong obstacles to Hamlet's major action of avenging his murdered father: Claudius conspires to have Hamlet killed, Polonius tries to spy on him, Rosencrantz and Guildenstern try to betray him, and Hamlet himself has his own inner obstacles which come out in the famous soliloquys. It's to Hamlet's credit that he manages to overcome every one of these obstacles and finally achieve his major action at the end of the play.

5. *The greatness of any action depends on how much is at stake.* In *Hamlet* there are the highest stakes imaginable—it's not only a life and death situation for Hamlet himself, and not only does the entire welfare of Denmark depend on the successful outcome of Hamlet's action, but the existence of a moral order in the universe depends on whether Hamlet can avenge his murdered father and restore justice to the nature of things. Because these stakes are all so very great, an audience will care very much about what happens in the play.

These arc the ways in which the basic principles of dramatic action are operating in *Hamlet* to make it effective as a play. To be sure, there may be other approaches to the play which may probe more deeply into the philosophical aspects of the material, there may be interpretations which can account for the psychosexual motivations of the characters, and there may be literary appreciations of Shakespeare's great poetry and his "insights into human nature." But none of these approaches can begin to account for why the play works as well as it does onstage. And after all, in the theatre that's all that really matters.

We can keep right on applying these dramatic principles of dramatic writing to other plays—by Henrik Ibsen, Eugene O'Neill and Tennessee Williams. We will see the same use of actions and visuals and stakes in each of these plays:

1. In *A Doll's House* by Ibsen, Nora's major action is to leave a marriage in which she is not free to exist as a human being. The onstage visuals that embody this major action are the wedding rings that Nora and Helmer give back to each other, the traveling-bag that Nora has packed for herself, and the door she walks out of at the end of the play. The stakes of the play are not only the marriage vows of this husband and this wife, but the underlying premise of all marriage vows in the modern world —which accounts for why the play caused all hell to break loose when it was first produced, and can still ruffle a few tailfeathers in our own time each time it is performed.

2. In O'Neill's *Long Day's Journey Into Night,* Mary Tyrone's major action is to get back into a twilight dope haze as quickly as possible, which is why the other members of her family are on the verge of utter desperation. The onstage visuals that embody these actions are Jamie's fits of coughing, the bottle of bonded Bourbon, the fog that rolls in from the sound like a white curtain that is drawn outside the windows of the house, and the old-fashioned white satin wedding gown that Mary trails along the floor at her final entrance. The stakes of the play are overwhelmingly great for every member of the Tyrone family, and therefore they are also great for everyone in the audience as well.

3. In *Cat on a Hot Tin Roof* by Tennessee Williams, Maggie the Cat's major action is to get her husband Brick to make love to her so she can get pregnant and give the lie to the rest of the family. The onstage visuals are the big double bed which is slightly raked so that figures on it can be seen more easily, and Brick's crutch on which he hobbles about the stage, which embodies his denial of his role as husband and lover. The stakes are enormous for each character in the play: to confront his or her mendacity and find some way of overcoming the life of lies that has been going on for so long. Consequently the audience cares very much about the outcome of the play.

At this point we could mention a few examples of plays where these basic principles of actions, visuals, and stakes do *not* work as well as they should onstage. The most obvious example in the modern theatre is in George Bernard Shaw's four act play, *Man and Superman.* There is an interminable philosophical dialogue in the second half of act three called "Don Juan in Hell," in which the Devil, Don Juan, Dona Aña, and a statue of the Commander sit around and discuss the nature of life and love in an endless ramble that has neither action nor visuals nor stakes. It is a bravura display of epigrammatic wit and cosmic banter, and it may seem to some to be a daring diversion from the usual humdrum theatrical fare, but it can be hell on any audience that has to sit through three and a half hours of the entire uncut play.

And our own commercial Broadway theatre has an odd way of spawning ersatz "problem" plays which purport to deal with crucial and controversial social or moral issues, and these plays may seem to have authentic actions and visuals and stakes until one thinks about them afterwards and realizes they are nothing but a lot of theatrical rhetoric and artifice. Robert Anderson's *Tea and Sympathy* was one such play, where a teenage boy in boarding school is going through a harried time and the wife of his housemaster takes it upon herself to help him grow up and become a man. The play may be moving enough in its own way, but one senses the subtext is puffed out of all proportion to the onstage situation, so the end result is more a conversation piece than it is an example of serious dramatic writing. The same is true of more recent plays like *Equus* by Peter Shaffer, in which a psychiatrist is trying to find out why a seventeen year old boy put out the eyes of six horses, and *Agnes of God* by John Pielmeier, in which a young nun is found unconscious in her room and a dead infant is in the waste basket, strangled with its own umbilical cord. Both these plays begin with a catastrophe that has already taken place offstage, and all the characters onstage are earnestly trying to figure out why it had to happen. But instead of a strong Sherlock Holmes "whodunit" action of discovery, these plays are filled with discussion and detours and digressions as one of the central characters tries to figure out "whydunit." And while this may give an audience the illusion of seriousness, it is the very opposite of having a strong dramatic action that advances over the course of a play to a necessary and engaging climax.

Also there are all those so-called "verse plays" by any number of major poets who thought it might be a nice idea to try and write for the theatre. The result, for the most part, is a body of precious work that often resembles the masques that were written for special court performances, in which brilliant poetry takes the place of dramatic action—as in the plays of Shelley, William Butler Yeats, Edna St.Vincent Millay, Robert Frost, Robert Lowell, Wallace Stevens, and Dylan Thomas. In many of these plays the language may be marvelously soaring and resonant and responsive, but invariably the poetry takes precedence over dramatic actions, visuals, and stakes, and therefore these plays generally tend to founder on their own eloquence. Because in all good dramatic writing, language must always be seen as a consequence of dramatic action, and that's why almost all the memorable speeches in the plays of Shakespeare are always the result of some great underlying dramatic action in the subtext. To be sure, in our modern theatre we have had some poets who learned to subordinate language to strong subtext actions, as T. S. Eliot did in *The Cocktail Party*, and Maxwell Anderson in *Winterset*, and Christopher Fry in *The Lady's Not For Burning*, and Archibald MacLeish in *J.B.*, and Robinson Jeffers in his translation of *Medea*. In these plays at least we can feel the powerful fusion of poetry and dramatic action.

As we said at the beginning of this chapter, the most important thing for a playwright to realize about playwriting is that there is a crucial difference between dramatic and narrative writing. Plays are not novels, the stage is not the printed page, and no matter how much talent, verbal skill, and background experience one may have for narrative writing, unless one has mastered the basic principles of dramatic action, visuals, and stakes, one cannot even hope to know how to *read* a good play intelligently, let alone try to *write* one that will play effectively onstage.

ADVICE FOR PLAYWRIGHTS

Dramatic writing has to have strong actions and visuals and stakes—as well as obstacles to get dramatic conflict started. And these basic principles of dramatic writing have to be actively practiced by the playwright until they become second nature to him.

SUGGESTED READING

Aristotle: *Poetics* (any edition).

EXERCISES

1. Create a character and give this character a strong action. Create a visual that will embody this character's action. Then create an obstacle that will keep this character from getting what he wants. Decide how much is at stake for this character. Now write all this down in a brief scene of about five to ten pages and see what happens.

2. Go back to the scene in the first exercise and try changing the obstacles so there will be stronger things for the character to overcome. Also try shifting the stakes of the character's action, so they will be much greater. Now write all this down in another brief scene of about five to ten pages and see what happens.

3. Choose one of your favorite novels and try writing a brief dramatic version of one of the chapters, providing the appropriate dramatic actions, visuals, obstacles, and stakes, and see what happens.

CHAPTER 2

THE STAGE IS A VISUAL AREA

The most important thing about the stage is that it is a visual area—that is, it is something to be looked at, it is something to be seen.

The very word "theatre" comes from the early Greek "theatron" which means "a seeing place," from "theasthai," "to see." This may seem to be a terribly obvious truth to us, but these terribly obvious truths are the things we tend to keep overlooking and forgetting.

In fact we can pinpoint the first historical period in which this terribly obvious truth about the stage being a visual area was first overlooked and forgotten. That was in the Roman theatre, when the word for "theatre" became "auditorium" or "hearing place" —which is a considerable shift away from the Greek idea of theatre as "a seeing place." And in this Roman theatre, the visual aspect of the stage tended to degenerate into stock stage props like lopped off heads and hands, and the plays began to develop a lot of oratorical

21

long speeches. But there were no strong dramatic actions or vivid onstage visuals, such as there had been in the Greek theatre.

And this was not true theatre, where the stage is a visual area which is there to be seen, and plays convey their major actions through the onstage visuals.

Another way of saying all this is to paraphrase the old saying, "One picture is worth a thousand words." We could say that in the theatre, one good onstage visual is worth a thousand oratorical speeches. And this means that a playwright must train himself to present things that are seen, things that can be looked at, things that will show what is happening onstage. In other words, the playwright must train himself to translate all his verbal narrative impulses into vivid living onstage visuals.

"Don't *tell* me—*show* me." That is our basic dramatic principle.

One good way for a playwright to train himself in this visual way of thinking, is to imagine that there is somebody sitting in the audience who is hard of hearing. This person does not understand a single word of dialogue or any of the long expository speeches. Even so, this person should still be able to look at the stage and follow the course of the action of a play, simply by seeing what is taking place, visually, onstage.

This is an excellent exercise for a playwright, and one can test it by looking at some of the greatest plays ever written, to find out whether there are enough vivid onstage visuals to communicate the ongoing action of the play to someone in the audience who may not be able to follow the onstage language.

Think of *Oedipus Rex*. From his first entrance onstage, we see Oedipus hobbling around on his clubfoot as he keeps asking questions about some infant who had his ankles broken in childhood. Or think of the first time we see Hamlet dressed entirely in black, while all the other onstage characters are in their colorful court costumes. Or think of Laura in *The Glass Menagerie*, with her slight limp as she handles the delicate glass creatures of her menagerie collection.

All these great plays are so remarkably visual, that even if we did not understand the language of the dialogue, we would still be able to get a very real sense of what was happening simply by seeing the onstage visuals.

Of course a playwright has to train himself to master this use of onstage visuals, and that may take some time. In fact we can see a good example of a playwright teaching himself the appropriate use of onstage visuals in the life work of one of our great modern playwrights, George Bernard Shaw. Shaw tells us in his dedication to *Man and Superman* in 1903, that a friend's favorite jibe at him was that what Shaw called "drama" was nothing but *explanation*—that is, Shaw had not yet learned to curb his strong narrative impulse to *tell* an audience something, and consequently his plays were witty and verbose and intelligent but they were not yet truly dramatic. And Shaw's friend had a point. Anyone who has ever sat through a complete production of *Man and Superman* can attest to a certain weariness that sets in during all that endless talk-talk-talk, especially during the interminable "Don Juan in Hell" sequence, which is nothing but a nonstop philosophical meditation on the meaning of life, love, and procreation in the universe. This sequence is mercifully cut from most productions of *Man and Superman*, because while it contains some of Shaw's most brilliant writing, the stage is no place to allow such inordinate speechmaking.

But by the time Shaw came to write *Saint Joan* in 1924, he had learned his lesson that theatre is no place for making endless narrative speeches of "explanation." His *Saint Joan* is a masterpiece of actions that are embodied in brilliantly chosen onstage visuals. The visuals in the opening three scenes of *Saint Joan* show us there is something truly extraordinary about this seventeen year old girl:

1. In the first scene, the steward complains the hens are not laying eggs—but after Joan appears onstage, the steward comes running in with a basket that is overflowing with five dozen eggs. We *see* the effect Joan has had on everything and everyone around her.

2. In the second scene, the Dauphin hides himself among his courtiers and Bluebeard tries to pass himself off as the Dauphin—but Joan moves right past Bluebeard and the rest of the courtiers until she can locate the real Dauphin in his hiding place.

3. In the third scene, Dunois is standing at Orleans with a pennon streaming in a strong east wind—but after Joan appears onstage, we see the pennon change direction and begin streaming in a strong west wind.

These three opening scenes of *Saint Joan* are all we need to see that Joan is everything her followers claim her to be. And Shaw does it by using vivid onstage visuals, instead of long narrative speeches of "explanation."

Now we should try to define what we mean by the word *visual*. What is a visual?

We could answer the question by saying what a visual is *not*. A visual is not just a cigarette or a paper clip or an ostrich plume or a stick of lipstick. These things are just stage props and accessories. And by the same token, a visual is not just a sight gag or some fast costume change or a lot of flashy sets, which are nothing but claptrap and paraphernalia and stage "business." And a visual is not a nineteenth century melodramatic device in which the villain steps forward to the footlights and twirls his mustache and opens his coat and shows the audience that he has the deed to the family homestead —that's nothing but illustration and indication.

A visual has to be more organic to the play than any of these things.

A dramatic visual is any object or article or part of the stage itself that can be seen as the embodiment of a major action. Another way of saying this is: A visual is a dramatic metaphor that is the immediate representation of what the onstage characters are all about.

The clubfoot of Oedipus that causes him to hobble around onstage—Hamlet's "inky cloak" of mourning black—Laura's slight limp and delicate figurines in *The Glass Menagerie*—all these are vivid living onstage visuals that tell us more about the characters in the plays than any number of fancy speeches about the blind arrogance of Oedipus, Hamlet's grief at the death of his murdered father, or Laura's psychic frailty.

How does one go about choosing an appropriate visual for a play?

It takes a special way of thinking, a special way of imagining, to come up with appropriate onstage visuals. Aristotle in the *Poetics* says that to be a master of metaphor is the surest sign of genius, and he also says it's the one thing that can't be taught—you either have this genius for metaphor or you don't.

It sounds like the most anyone else can do is explain what visual metaphors are all about, and then point you in the right direction and wish you a lot of luck. But in reality one can offer a good deal more than this, in the way of useful guidelines and ongoing exercises to help develop someone's ability to create vivid living onstage visuals.

And the first thing we'd say to any beginning playwright about how to go about creating good onstage visuals is: Don't be shy about it. Too many playwrights are afraid of seeming too "theatrical," completely forgetting the fact that they are, indeed, writing for the *theatre!* The stage is a visual area and the theatre is "a seeing place," and the one thing one must not be in the theatre is too tame and safe and literary. One has to find onstage visuals that will *show* the major actions of the characters. And if this seems too reckless and flamboyant and outrageous to any playwright, then he'd better shake himself loose from such restraints and begin practicing the search for appropriate and, yes, theatrical visuals.

The best way for a playwright to go about finding the right visuals to use in his plays is the same kind of technique that an actor uses when he does physical object exercises. An actor will play with an object endlessly, turning it over in his hands, improvising all the different things he can do with it, until sooner or later he hits on the one precisely right way of using the physical object onstage.

That's a good way for the playwright to proceed. He should let his imagination wander aimlessly and endlessly over all the various physical objects that may be onstage, and he should try to think of all the different ways these physical objects might be used. He may feel pretty foolish doing this, and the various uses of the objects may strike him as reckless and flamboyant and outrageous, but sooner or later he will hit on the one true visual that will embody the major actions of his character.

Here is an example of an exercise to find the right onstage visual:

> Four characters are shipwrecked on a desert island. Three characters have given up all hope of ever being rescued, but the fourth character refuses to give up hope.

What sort of visuals will express these four characters? We don't want to write a lot of long-winded speeches for the characters to deliver about their various attitudes—we want to find onstage visuals that will express all four characters at a single glance.

We should begin by saying that there is no "right" answer to this challenge. Different playwrights will come up with different visuals to express this situation, and that's as it should be. All that matters is that the visuals be clear and sharp and theatrical.

Well, here's our own choice of visuals for the dramatic situation we described:

> The three characters who have given up all hope have dug three holes in the sand, and they are half buried in these holes. But the fourth character who refuses to give up hope has taken off his shirt and tied

it to the top of a palm tree, and he stays standing onstage and looking out towards the sea.

This may not be the greatest solution one could come up with, but at least it's clear and sharp and anyone in the audience could tell immediately what the four characters are all about. And that's what really matters.

This kind of improvisational exercise is not as difficult as it sounds, especially when we remember that children are continually creating visuals in their play. Kids can pick up a pillow or a blanket or the branch of a tree and immediately transform these things into living embodiments of some imaginary action. A doll or a toy gun or a tent will turn children into mothers or soldiers or explorers, and playwrights have to train themselves to remember the way they used to play as children, with free and easy make-believe, to achieve this purely visual state of being. It's a little like being a stage magician, as Tom Wingfield reminds us in the opening lines of *The Glass Menagerie:*

> Yes, I have tricks in my pocket, I have things up my sleeve. But I am the opposite of a stage magician. He gives you illusion that has the appearance of truth. I give you truth in the pleasant guise of illusion.[1]

These "illusions" of the playwright are his dramatic visuals, which embody the major actions of his characters.

Let's take another specific example. Right now you are reading this book about playwriting. If you were acting in a play right now, this book would be just one more stage prop, like a lamp or an ashtray or a telephone. But suppose the character you're portraying onstage has to take an examination in one hour, in which he will be tested on everything that's contained in this book. And let's suppose a great deal depends on your character's getting a good grade on the exam, because his whole future career depends on it. Now this book is no longer a mere stage prop, it has suddenly become a dramatic visual that embodies your character's major action, which is to pass the exam. Even now as you read this paragraph perhaps you can feel yourself beginning to clutch this book a bit more intensely, as if you wanted to absorb as much of what it contains as possible. Or perhaps you suddenly feel like throwing this book against the wall—that would be another good use of the book as an onstage visual. In any event, you are now aware that you have transformed this book from being a mere stage prop to being a vivid living onstage visual.

You can play games like this with anything—a pair of scissors, a cup of coffee, a pair of boots. Nothing is too unimportant or too trivial that you cannot endow it with some major action and transform it into a living onstage visual.

Of course it will take practice before this ability to create appropriate visuals will begin to come freely and easily. Meanwhile one can always read plays by other playwrights and see how they approached the problem of visuals. Following are a few examples of outstanding onstage visuals from some of the greatest plays ever written:

1. In the *Agamemnon* of Aeschylus, the play begins with a strong visual—a watchman is on a tower, and he is weary with waiting for the news of the end of the Trojan war. Suddenly a bright light appears in the distance to announce the end of the war, and the audience sees this light before the watchman does, so the audience will see the watchman seeing the light and share in his discovery of the good news.

Then Agamemnon enters onstage in a horse-drawn chariot, with the slave girl Cassandra beside him, and this horse and chariot will remain standing onstage for the rest of the play.

Then Clytemnestra orders her handmaidens to spread a blood-red carpet along the ground for Agamemnon to walk up to the palace doors, and the audience knows that once he sets foot on this carpet, he will be going towards his death.

At the end of the play, the palace doors are thrown open and the dead bodies of Agamemnon and Cassandra are seen lying inside the palace.

All these visuals are embodiments of the major action of the play —Clytemnestra's desire to kill the homecoming Agamemnon. It is one of the greatest visual plays ever written.

2. In the *Electra* by Sophocles, Electra is mourning the death of her brother Orestes, holding an urn in which she thinks are the ashes of Orestes. Orestes, disguised as a shepherd, comes in and sits beside her. Electra continues to hold the urn as she mourns for Orestes, as Orestes looks on. Finally Orestes reveals himself to Electra by showing her a ring that belonged to their father Agamemnon, and when Electra sees the ring, she recognizes her brother Orestes and she sets the urn aside.

This is one of the greatest recognition scenes in all theatre, and it achieves its extraordinary power by using the great onstage visuals of the urn, the disguise, and the ring.

3. Shakespeare included outstanding visuals which embody the major actions of his characters in almost every scene he ever wrote. These are some of the more memorable visuals:

Richard III shows his crippled body to the audience at the beginning of *Richard III*.

Hamlet plays with a skull before he realizes it belonged to someone he knew in childhood.

Macbeth sees an imaginary dagger in mid-air.

Bassanio has to choose from among three caskets in *The Merchant of Venice.*

The black moor Othello strangles the white Desdemona.

Bottom wears an ass's head in *A Midsummer Night's Dream.*

A young woman is disguised as a young man in *Twelfth Night, All's Well That Ends Well, As You Like It,* and *The Merchant of Venice.*

The French ambassadors present Henry V with a set of tennis balls in *Henry V.*

Marc Antony reveals the stab wounds on the corpse of Julius Caesar to the Romans.

Lear rages at the storm on the heath in *King Lear.*

Cleopatra attaches asps to each of her breasts in *Antony and Cleopatra.*

Hermione is transformed into a statue in *The Winter's Tale.*

If we didn't know any of these plays, we'd say the above list is filled with a lot of theatrical, flamboyant, and reckless visuals. The point is that these visuals are all clear and sharp and powerful onstage, and they do the job that has to be done in the play. In fact it's an extraordinary thing that for all his verbal brilliance and poetic genius, Shakespeare rarely trusted language to do the work that a good onstage visual can do. Each of the above visuals helps to embody some major action of character, and it also helps to advance the major action of the play itself.

4. In *The Cherry Orchard* by Chekhov, the cherry blossoms themselves are vivid onstage visuals for the brief fleeting moment of life itself. In the first and fourth acts of the play, we see the cherry trees continuously through the windows as the action of the play takes place. The stage directions read quite simply:

> *The windows of the room are shut, but through them the cherry trees can be seen in blossom . . .*

5. In *Long Day's Journey Into Night* by Eugene O'Neill, the onstage visual is the fog that rolls in from the sound like a white curtain drawn outside the windows of the house. There is another haunting visual that is used in the last act of the play, when Mary Tyrone makes her final appearance. Here is the stage direction:

> *MARY appears in the doorway. She wears a sky-blue dressing gown over her night dress, dainty slippers with pompoms on her bare feet . . . Over one arm, carried neglectfully, trailing on the floor, as if she had forgotten she held it, is an old-fashioned white satin wedding gown, trimmed with duchesse lace . . .*[2]

O'Neill goes on to describe Mary Tyrone's eyes as wide, glistening like jewels. This is a devastating visual that confirms the worst fears of the Tyrone men—that Mary is on dope once again.

6. In *Our Town* by Thornton Wilder, the entire stage becomes a visual in the third act, as the dead people of Grovers Corners sit on chairs facing the audience, and a funeral is about to take place. The stage directions read:

> *From left center, at the back of the stage, comes a procession. Four men carry a casket, invisible to us. All the rest are under umbrellas. One can vaguely see: DR. GIBBS, GEORGE, the WEBBS, etc. They gather about a grave in the back center of the stage, a little to the left of center. Pause. Suddenly EMILY appears from among the umbrellas. She is wearing a white dress. Her hair is down her back, and tied by a white ribbon like a little girl. She comes slowly, gazing wondering at the dead, a little dazed. She stops halfway and smiles faintly. After looking at the mourners for a moment, she walks slowly to the vacant chair beside MRS. GIBBS and sits down.*[3]

These stark visuals of the black umbrellas and the sudden appearance of Emily in her white dress, show us all we need to know about life and death in *Our Town*. Even so, we are always deeply moved by the overwhelming power of the last great visual of this play, when George comes onstage and throws himself down full length onstage before the seated figure of the dead Emily.

We could go on and list other outstanding visuals in other plays, but the basic point is made: the stage is a visual area, the theatre is "a seeing place," and characters and actions have to be embodied in living vivid onstage visuals. And one should not be shy about this—sometimes one has to relax and be as flamboyant as possible to arrive at the appropriate onstage visuals that are absolutely right for one's own play.

ADVICE FOR PLAYWRIGHTS

Train yourself to think visually so you can translate major actions into vivid onstage visuals.

SUGGESTED READING

Uta Hagen: *Respect For Acting*, Macmillan, 1973.

EXERCISES

1. Pick up three objects that are around you right now, and try to endow them with a major action so they will become vivid onstage visuals. Then write a brief scene that uses all three of these visuals.

2. Write three brief scenes that have visuals to show the following major actions:
   a. someone wants to kill someone else.
   b. someone wants to love someone else.
   c. someone wants to get power over someone else.

3. Write a brief scene which contains a visual for an entire group of characters onstage, embodying a major action for all of them.

CHAPTER 3

DRAMA IS ACTION

Action is the heart and soul of drama.

We've been using that word "action" a good deal, now we ought to try and define it.

It's easy enough for us to say what an action is *not*. An action is not a lot of "stage business" or "activity." Someone may cross the stage to light a cigarette, but that's not necessarily an action; it may just be a piece of blocking. And there are plenty of plays where a lot of characters keep running around all over the stage, but that doesn't necessarily mean there's any real action. It could just be like crosstown traffic on a city street—it looks busy, but it's not going anywhere really important.

Dramatic action, on the other hand, is the life of a play. Drama *is* action—without action, there can be no drama at all.

Very well then, what is an action?

A dramatic action is a want, a need, a desire, a going for something. This is the same thing as saying that it is an objective:

31

one's action is one's objective, it is what one wants, it is what one has to have.

Oedipus wants to discover the cause of the moral pollution in Thebes, that is his action, it is his objective, it is what he has to have. Hamlet wants to avenge his murdered father, that is his action, it is what he has to have. Vladimir and Estragon want to wait for Godot, that is their action, it is their objective, it is what they have to have.

These are all strong clear actions, and that is why these plays play as well as they do onstage. In fact, we could say everything else that happens in these plays is secondary to these strong major actions.

Actions begin when someone asks: what do I want? What is my objective? What do I have to have, in this beat or scene or play? And the answer always follows: I want this, or I want that, or I want some other thing.

No one can try to create an action by trying to think about it—that only leads to intellectual and literary "ideas," not really dramatic actions. One is better off getting up onstage and performing a part oneself, so then one can feel it in one's deepest being, which is where all real dramatic action comes from.

I want something, I have to have something—that is the basis of all dramatic action.

If something or someone gets in the way of my getting what I want, that is an obstacle that I will have to overcome. We'll deal with obstacles in the next chapter.

How badly do I want what I want? That introduces the stakes of my action, and we'll deal with stakes in chapter five.

The Russian director Richard Boleslavsky describes dramatic action from a very unusual point of view:

> Look at that tree. It is the protagonist of all arts; it is an ideal structure of action. Upward movement and sideways resistance, balance and growth.[1]

Imagine someone looking at a tree and seeing it as an example of dramatic action! Yet Boleslavsky trained himself to see action everywhere, because he was an actor and a director and a teacher of acting. And he goes on to say that the playwright is the hidden action within that tree: "he is the sap that flows and feeds the whole." That is, the playwright is always the initiator and the mainstream of dramatic action.

All playwriting grows out of an understanding of this action. Aristotle says in the *Poetics* that all tragedy is the imitation of an action. That is, the actors onstage are not performing real actions like killing people or crossing the Alps or falling in love, but miming these actions for the sake of the play and the playwright who wrote these actions. But they *believe* the actions they are playing onstage, and that is what makes the audience believe the actions also.

Action is the key to creating all powerful dramatic writing. This may surprise some Shakespearean scholars, but dramatic actions are much more important than language, no matter how brilliant or extraordinary that language may be. In fact, the dramatic actions are the reason why the language is as great as it is. One can test this by thinking of any great speech from any of Shakespeare's plays: "To be or not to be" or "If it were done when 'tis done" or "Our revels now are ended." The poetry in these speeches is undeniably great, yet what makes such speeches truly dramatic is the remarkably great action that underlies each of these speeches. In "To be or not to be" Hamlet is contemplating whether or not he should kill himself; in "If it were done when 'tis done" Macbeth is trying to decide whether or not he should kill the king; and with "Our revels now are ended" Prospero is renouncing his magical powers and returning to the world of merely mortal affairs. Because these underlying actions are so great, the characters almost inevitably speak in powerfully great poetry.

Shakespeare has Hamlet say as much in his advice to the players:

Suit the action to the word, and the word to the action.[2]

That is to say, dramatic action and language have to be suited to one another, simultaneously, so they will seem to be one and the same thing. Therein lies the secret of dramatic writing.

Action is also the key to creating powerful characters. Actors know this, when they talk about "the magic if"—"If I were king, I would do such and such" or "If I loved you, I would do anything for you." Dramatic action always has this element of the hypothetical, of things that *might* happen, the conditional, the subjunctive. That's why we make "plays," because we are "playing" with reality, we are imagining what would happen "if" we had certain actions, where they might take us, and what they might make us do. Aristotle says this in the *Poetics:*

A probable impossibility is preferable to an improbable possibility.[3]

This looks like doubletalk but what Aristotle means is that what *might* happen is always better than what *could* happen. Similarly, what *might* have happened in the past is more interesting, dramatically, than what actually *did* happen, which is merely history. This explains why historical plays are so boring, unless a playwright takes some license, as Shakespeare did, and writes about what might have happened in the mind and heart of the character, instead of what historical records tell us did happen.

If action is the key to creating powerful dramatic writing and dramatic characters, then actions should be *clear* and *strong* and *right there* in the dramatic text.

1. Actions should be *clear*. No actor is ever going to be caught onstage without having a clear dramatic action which is his whole reason for being there. The first thing any actor asks when he picks up a playscript is: what is my action? what do I want? what is my objective? Now, if an actor is looking for his action in that playscript, the playwright had better have put a clear action there for him to find, otherwise the actor will make up some action of his own to play onstage, and that action may be something that the playwright did not intend.

There is an old joke in the theatre, that if an actor doesn't know what his action is supposed to be, he can always play that he has to go to the bathroom. At least that will give the actor a strong sense of urgency that will pass for an impressive dramatic action.

It is better, of course, for the playwright to set down a clear action in the text, so the actor will not have to improvise his action. In fact, most great playwrights, like Sophocles and Shakespeare, will invariably state what a character's action is in the very opening lines of every major speech. For example, Hamlet's opening soliloquy "O that this too too solid flesh would melt" reveals right away that Hamlet's clear action at the beginning of the play is that he wants to die—and this is the clear action that any actor would have to play in that first act, before Hamlet encounters Horatio and the tower guards who lead him to his father's ghost.

2. Actions should be *strong*. Without strong action, characters are not playable. The worst example of a character who does not have a strong action is a neurotic, and that's why neurotics always play so badly onstage. Because whatever their psychological problems may be, one characteristic of neurotics is that they don't know what they really want. And that violates our rule that all dramatic characters have to have strong clear actions. Therefore neurotics will play weakly, and any audience will get impatient with them. Good heavens, the audience will say, if this character can't make up his mind about what he wants, he'd better go off

and figure it out, and not come back until he knows what he wants. Because in the theatre it's better to have a character who is a vicious murderer, like Richard III, than a harmless neurotic, because at least Richard III knows he wants to commit a lot of vicious murders, and that's more dramatic for an audience to watch than some neurotic who just stands around wondering what he wants.

3. Actions should be *right there* in the text. Finally, the playwright has to beware of putting his dramatic actions in the stage directions, with all sorts of instructions to the actors about how so and so wants such and such. For example:

> *(JOHN enters.*   *He wants to marry ALICE but he does not know how to go about it so he has decided to kill her instead. In this scene JOHN wants to get it all over with as quickly as possible. The actor playing JOHN should play him with passion and pathos.)*

That is no way to go about dramatic writing! All the actions in this stage direction have to be developed strongly and clearly in the dialogue of the play itself, otherwise it's pointless to spell out the results in a silly stage direction like the one above. Besides, most actors always cross out stage directions from their working scripts so they will not be diverted from their task of giving onstage life to the dialogue. That's why it's so crucial for a playwright to put the dramatic actions right there in the text itself, and not describe them in the stage directions.

Actions, then, should be strong and clear and right there in the text. Granted this, how should a playwright go about locating strong clear actions that will be appropriate for his play?

This isn't always easy—in fact, it's probably the most difficult part of playwriting. Without strong clear actions there can be no drama, but one can't fake these actions, they have to come somehow out of the deepest core of the characters, which means they have to come most deeply out of the playwright himself.

The one thing a playwright can't do is impose an action on a character from the outside. He can't just arbitrarily say "I'll make so-and-so want to do such-and-such." That's what we'd call an external approach to playwriting, like using a cookie cutter to excise a predetermined shape and form, and it never works. It's much better for the playwright to allow a character to tell the playwright what the character wants. And the best way of doing this is for the playwright to open a notebook and begin writing, "My name is such and such and I want . . ."—and then to keep writing, using the voice of the character. A simple exercise like this will usually take the playwright right into the major action of the character, and then he can make all the appropriate decisions about that major action: how much depends on the character's getting what he wants, what obstacles are in his way, and how much does he really want it.

And once a dramatic action begins to emerge out of the voice of one of the characters, the playwright may recognize the action as one of the age-old recurrent actions in the theatre. Because there are certain major actions that do keep coming back again and again, in all plays and in all playwriting, and so it might be useful here to make a list of some of these recurrent actions:

1. *Discovery Action.* Aristotle calls this the greatest of all dramatic actions and he's probably right, because this discovery action is the major action of such great plays from *Oedipus Rex* right down to every detective story, murder mystery, and whodunit ever written, where the chief interest is to find something out. We watch as someone, usually the protagonist, passes from a state of ignorance to a state of knowledge about something.

In the modern theatre, one of the most moving examples of a discovery action occurs in *The Miracle Worker* by William Gibson, in the last scene of the play, when the child Helen Keller discovers the relation between the spelling of the word "water" and the sensation of water being poured out onto her hand from the water pump. At that instant the child passes from a state of ignorance to a state of knowledge, as she discovers the connection between language and reality. It is an overwhelmingly powerful moment for us also, as we witness this discovery by the blind-deaf-mute child.

2. *Seduction Action.* Someone wants to get someone to do something. Sexual seduction is the most obvious example of this action, and in the pursuit of a sexual seduction some characters will do just about anything to achieve their objective—they will flatter, lie, brag, threaten, beg, blackmail, cajole, sometimes even promise marriage! But this seduction action can operate on many other levels besides the purely sexual. It will be behind any major persuasion or con job or sales pitch with which one person is trying to get another person to do something.

A good example of non-sexual seduction action is the way Iago tries to seduce Othello into thinking that Desdemona has been unfaithful to him. It takes a long time—almost four acts of the whole play—for Iago to succeed in this seduction action, but when he finally does achieve his objective, Othello is on the brink of madness and homicidal outrage, and he does finally strangle Desdemona because of Iago's seduction action.

3. *Goal Action.* Someone can want something very specific, like money or power or status, and this will function strongly as a major dramatic action. A banker wants a million dollars; Macbeth wants to be king; a woman wants to go to London—all these goals will make for strong actions in the characters who pursue them, so long as the characters go after their objectives strongly and clearly.

4. *Revenge Action.* For some reason, audiences will always accept some-one's desire to get even with someone else as one of the strongest dramatic actions. Whether in classical tragedy like the *Oresteia* of Aeschy-lus, or in a blood tragedy like *The Spanish Tragedy* by Thomas Kyd, or in a play like *Hamlet* by William Shakespeare, any lone individual's wish for revenge will always play strongly onstage.

Similarly, family vendettas and blood feuds like that between the Montagues and the Capulets in *Romeo and Juliet,* or the Hatfields and the McCoys in our mid-Atlantic states; or the dead fish that are sent out as hit contracts among the Mafia; or the lethal street brawls between rival gangs in *West Side Story*—this type of revenge action will always be powerful and engage our deepest sympathies and identification with someone who wants to get even with someone else.

5. *Escape Action.* Someone says, "I want to get the hell out of here!" It could be a spectacular jail break, or a flight from a totalitarian state, or a psychological escape action as when Nora walks out on her bad marriage in Ibsen's *A Doll's House.* Whatever the form, an escape action will always involve an audience strongly if it is pursued strongly.

6. *Testing Action.* This is a common action that takes place every day of our lives: we test the people around us, to find out where they are coming from. And when the stakes are high enough, the testing action works strongly in spy stories and plays that take place under an oppressive tyranny, when characters have to find out whether other characters are on the same side or not. This happens with many of the minor characters in *Macbeth* such as Lennox and the Lord, and also in *The Private Life of The Master Race* by Bertolt Brecht. One's life can depend on finding out whether one trusts someone else, and the only way of finding out whether the other person is trustworthy or not is to test that person in as many ways as possible.

7. *"Getting to Know You" Action.* This is a variation of the seduction action and the testing action, but it is a distinct action in its own right. Someone is trying to get to know someone else. It's not necessary for there to be a seduction involved, or very high stakes—one is simply trying to break the ice. An excellent example of this "getting to know you" action takes place in the park bench scene in Molnar's *Liliom,* and also in the soda fountain scene in act two of Thornton Wilder's *Our Town.*

8. *Crossroads Choice Action.* This is an action in which a character tries to decide between two major actions that lie ahead of him. It gives the illusion that a character is able to step back and freely choose which major action he will pursue in the play.

Hamlet does this in the famous "To be or not to be" speech, when he seems to be trying to decide whether to kill himself or not:

> To be, or not to be: that is the question:
> Whether 'tis nobler in the mind to suffer

The slings and arrows of outrageous fortune,
Or to take arms against a sea of troubles,
And by opposing end them? . . .[4]

Similarly, Macbeth has a crossroads action in his "If it were done when 'tis done" speech, in which he seems to be questioning whether he should kill King Duncan or not:

If it were done, when 'tis done, then 'twere well
It were done quickly; if th'assassination
Could trammel up the consequence, and catch,
With his surcease, success; that but this blow
Might be the be-all and the end-all. . . . here,
But here, upon this bank and shoal of time,
We'd jump the life to come. But in these cases
We still have judgement here; that we but teach
Bloody instructions, which, being taught, return
To plague th'inventor . . .[5]

This crossroads choice action is extremely perilous, as it tends to make a major character appear to be neurotic and unable to make up his own mind about which major action he should pursue. Indeed, both of the above speeches are notoriously difficult for any actor to deliver onstage, and it has nothing to do with the speeches being world-famous, or consisting of exalted poetry—it is because the character seems to be questioning whether or not he should continue on with his major action, and for an actor to play that form of detached self-examination removes him from the through line of the major action and makes him seem less dramatic and motivated.

9. *Reprise Action.* Just as in some musicals a composer writes a "reprise" number to restate the important melodies that have taken place in the course of the musical, so in a play sometimes a playwright will have a character restate the important circumstances and stakes that pertain to his dramatic situation. This happens most conspicuously in *Hamlet,* when Hamlet keeps going back over his major action and tries to remind himself of why he should do what he has to do:

O, Vengeance!
Why, what an ass am I. This is most brave,
That I, the son of a dear father murder'd,
Prompt'd to my revenge by heaven and hell,
Must, like a whore, unpack my heart with words,
And fall a-cursing, like a very drab,
A scullion! . . .[6]

The above list of recurrent actions does not exhaust all the possible major actions one can use in playwriting, but it does include the most common major actions that keep coming back again and again in almost all plays.

In addition to these major actions, there are a few more sophisticated minor actions that can occur in playwriting. Some of these minor actions are like the tricky gambits or ploys that people use in the games they play with each other in real life, to manipulate and maneuver situations. That does not make them any less valid as dramatic actions—in fact, if a playwright can reproduce them convincingly, it should cause a shudder of recognition in an audience. Following is a list of some of these more sophisticated minor actions:

1. *False Action.* A character indicates his major action is one thing, whereas in fact the major action is really another thing. The audience may or may not be aware that it is a false action, and indeed, sometimes the character himself may or may not be aware that it is a false action.

At the beginning of Shakespeare's play, Richard III announces to the audience that his major action is to kill just about everyone onstage and prove what a villain he is, yet to everyone onstage he pretends he is an extraordinarily virtuous person. Here the audience is aware of the falseness of Richard's action, so it will await the discovery by the other characters onstage that Richard is, indeed, a villain.

But in *The Three Sisters* by Chekhov, although the play begins with both Olga and Irina announcing that they want to go to Moscow, as it unfolds we in the audience realize that they are doing nothing much to advance that major action. We gradually realize it is a false action, and they must really want something else.

In almost every murder mystery or detective story, one of the characters will have to have a false action, because he is a criminal who is masking his real major action—otherwise there would be no mystery to unravel.

A playwright should realize that false actions are extremely tricky things to play with, and they must be carefully controlled and executed. Otherwise it may seem that a character is merely being neurotic and indecisive, which will simply confuse and alienate an audience.

2. *Withheld Action.* Like a false action, a withheld action is not immediately apparent as the major action of a character. This is because the withheld action is kept in reserve, to be revealed at some later time in the play. This will occur when it is not safe for a character to reveal his true major action, or when the character chooses to delay it for some other reason. An example of this occurs in *King Lear,* when both Edgar and the Fool have to withhold their true action of loyalty to Lear during the third and fourth acts of the play, while Lear is going mad on the heath. Only in the fifth act can both Edgar and the Fool reveal their major action, which is keeping allegiance to their King.

3. *Sleeper Action.* Like the withheld action and the false action, a sleeper action will be a temporarily suspended action which may look like another action. An example of this occurs in *The Duchess of Malfi* by John Webster, when Duke Ferdinand is described as someone who

> will seem to sleep o'the bench
> only to entrap offenders in their answers . . . [7]

In other words, Ferdinand pretends he is not paying attention to someone in his court, in order to catch him in some mistake so he can sentence him to death. Cats do this with mice all the time, as part of their playing with them.

4. *"Letting out Line" Action.* This term is taken from fishing, where one deliberately lets out line on a large fish and allows it to swim away, in order to tire the fish so it can then be pulled in more easily. This action seems to let the fish win the contest, whereas in reality it deceives the fish, making doubly sure that it will be netted. An example of this "letting out line" action occurs in *Othello*, when Iago seems to allow his insinuations to drift and wander, in order to let Othello "tire" himself out in seeming to see through them, before Iago begins to go to work in earnest on Othello.

5. *"Treading Water" Action.* This term is taken from swimming, where one sometimes stops swimming and treads water for a time, in order to conserve energy. It is an action, but only in reference to some other major action which one has temporarily suspended. An example of this "treading water" action is in *Hamlet,* where a good deal of the shorter soliloquys and asides are simply Hamlet's way of conserving energy before he goes back to his major action which is avenging his murdered father.

With all of these recurrent major and minor actions, the success of the actions will always depend on how strongly and clearly they are pursued by the dramatic characters, and on how much the characters really want the actions.

ADVICE FOR PLAYWRIGHTS

Train yourself to see drama as action, and try to create strong wants and desires and objectives for all the characters in your play.

SUGGESTED READING

Stanislavsky: *My Life in Art*, Meridian, 1948.

EXERCISES

1. Write a brief monologue for each of the following characters, giving each a strong clear major action:
   a. a medieval knight
   b. a heart surgeon
   c. a college dropout

2. Write a brief monologue for each of the following characters, developing the major action that is indicated:
   a. someone wants to run away from home
   b. someone wants to get back at someone else for something
   c. someone wants to win the love of someone else

3. Write a brief monologue in which you try to convince a Broadway producer that he ought to stage one of your own plays. Remember that this producer reads between 100 and 200 playscripts a week.

CHAPTER 4

OBSTACLES TO ACTION

Life is made up of eternal conflicts and competitions and contests. Dramatic action has to reflect this strong adversary relationship of forces that are endlessly opposed to one another.

Think of a rapidly rushing brook: it hurtles headlong down a mountainside, crashing around sudden turns, skimming over smooth stones, racing past glistening slippery rocks, going through narrow gulleys, bypassing inlets, as it keeps roaring forward with a cataclysmic force.

What is dramatic about this brook is its continuous overcoming of obstacles—because all real drama is the everlasting conflict of powerful actions coming up against strong obstacles.

An *obstacle* is any impediment, obstruction, hindrance, opposition, or stone wall barrier that stands in the way of someone's getting something that he wants. This obstacle may take the form of a person, a place, or a thing—or it could be an idea or a deadline or a

43

law or a snowstorm or an overdrawn bank account. It can be anything at all that sets itself up as an impediment to someone's getting something. But whatever it is, this obstacle is something that will have to be overcome, otherwise it will block any action that comes up against it.

In other words, that rapidly rushing brook will have to keep crashing and skimming and racing around all those obstacles, otherwise it will cease to be a rapidly rushing brook and instead it will become a muddy pond or a motionless lake. Now muddy ponds and motionless lakes have their own kind of lyric beauty, but they are no longer dramatically interesting in the same way the rapidly rushing brook was interesting. Because the muddy pond and the motionless lake don't satisfy our intense curiosity to watch what happens when a strong force comes up against a strong obstacle.

In fact one of the tricky riddles of early physics had to do with what happened when an "irresistible" force met an "immovable" object. It's sort of a nutty problem because, if you think about it, either that irresistible force will cease to be irresistible, or else that immovable object will cease to be immovable. Which is to say, either the action or the obstacle will have to yield, at the instant of impact. Even so, this riddle has a curious fascination for us, because of our own deep curiosity about such things—something in us wants to watch what will happen when these two things collide with one another. All hell might break loose, yet at least it will be a terrifically dramatic moment!

That's why major characters in drama are traditionally called the Protagonist and the Antagonist—to indicate their eternal opposition to one another, so that one will invariably serve as an obstacle to the other's action.

One can imagine how boring the world would be if there were no obstacles to our actions, if there were nothing but muddy ponds and motionless lakes. For example, one would think that our own erotic fantasies ought to be endlessly interesting to us, when we play them out on the stage of our own minds. But the fact is that our own erotic fantasies are really not all that interesting to us after a while, simply because there is no real obstacle to our wishes, and therefore there is no real dramatic tension.

One of our foremost actresses expresses this, from an acting point of view:

If I know what I want and can achieve my wishes readily without any problem, there is no drama. In tragedy and comedy and satire and farce—in anything that is worthy of the stage—conflict is at the root. Consequently, finding the obstacles to my objectives becomes imperative. I have to look for the crisis, the conflict, the clash of wills—the drama.[1]

In dramatic writing, obstacles can be located either *outside* a character, or *inside* a character.

Obstacles that are located *outside* a character can be anything that one comes up against outside oneself, that gets in the way of a major action.

Following is a list of external obstacles that one can come up against:

1. a stone wall—or a locked door, or any other physical impediment or barrier

2. a closed safe—or any other enclosure that has to be broken open

3. a mother-in-law—or a step-father, or any other family or clan relation that could cause complications and keep someone from doing something

4. a deadline—or any other time limit that keeps someone from doing something, or which enforces the doing of it by a certain time

5. the law—either God's law or man's law: some specific commandment or ordinance that prohibits someone from doing something

6. a gun at the head—or any other physical threat of injury or death if someone does or does not do something

7. a bully—or any other person whose mere physical presence can inspire terror and keep someone from doing something

8. fear of scandal—or threat of public exposure to shame or ridicule, to keep someone from doing something

9. a natural disaster—a tornado or a tidal wave or a hurricane or a typhoon or a blizzard or an avalanche or a flood or an earthquake or any other catastrophe that could keep someone from doing something

10. a disease—the plague or cholera or typhoid or a heart attack or a stroke, or any other physical illness that could keep someone from doing something

This is only a partial listing of the various external obstacles that can get in the way of a character's major action. The important thing is to understand the principle of an action coming up against an obstacle, thereby creating dramatic tension.

Think of the Big Bad Wolf, standing outside the locked doors of the three houses of the Three Little Pigs. At each door the Wolf says, "I'll huff and I'll puff and I'll blow your house down," and he does just that with the first two houses, until he comes to the third house that he cannot blow down. He has finally come up against an obstacle that is strong enough to resist his major action of huffing and puffing.

Or think of The Little Engine That Could, chugging its way up an enormous mountainside, saying to itself, "I think I can, I think I can, I think I can"—until the Little Engine gets up enough of a major action to overcome the external obstacle of that enormous mountainside.

Here we have two examples from nursery stories, one showing an obstacle successfully resisting a major action, and the other showing a major action finally overcoming an obstacle.

Following are some examples of external obstacles from a few great plays:

1. In Shakespeare's time, all the women onstage were played by young boys, so Shakespeare had to invent additional obstacles to keep the female characters from having that many intimate scenes with the male characters, since that would have struck an Elizabethan audience as ludicrous. Consequently in many of the comedies, the boys play females who disguise themselves as boys, a double obstacle. In *Romeo and Juliet,* the lovers are separated by the obstacle of physical distance during the balcony scene, so they have to work twice as hard to make their soaring vows of love. And in *Henry V,* Henry's courtship of Katharine is hindered by the fact that Henry does not understand French and Katharine does not understand English, so the lovers have to labor mightily to make their love understood to each other.

2. In *Death of a Salesman* by Arthur Miller, we see Willy Loman up against the obstacle of a ruthless dog-eat-dog world of salesmanship, and this obstacle eventually overwhelms any major action that Willy can find within himself.

3. In *Rhinoceros* by Eugene Ionesco, everyone in the world is turning into a rhinoceros except for the major character, and that is an obstacle the character has to confront and overcome if he is not to lose his own humanity.

A word of warning about external obstacles: If a playwright gets too heavy-handed with outside obstacles, they may so dominate a play that they will overshadow the major actions of the characters. When this happens, the result is melodrama of the worst kind, with a strong imposed premise clamped on top of a situation from the outside. In "cliffhanger" melodramas like *The Perils of Pauline,* there are too many external obstacles and they are too ludicrously contrived—the heroine is always floating downstream on huge ice cakes towards a roaring waterfall, or else she is tied to some railroad tracks and the 9:02 is just coming around the bend. When this happens we no longer look to the character for any major action in overcoming these obstacles. We just enjoy the character's last-minute ingenuity, which saves the day until the next cliffhanger situation comes along. But this is not the kind of dramatic tension that we associate with true theatre.

The second kind of obstacles are located *inside* a character, and they can be any inner reasons why a character should not keep on pursuing his major action. Following is a list of internal obstacles that one can come up against:

1. psychological obstacles—conscience or scruples or doubts or a conflict of loyalties or any other inner voice that keeps telling a character he should not do what he wants to do because it is wrong

2. psychiatric obstacles—insanity or any mental or emotional illness like amnesia that gets in the way of a character's doing what he wants to do

3. the so-called "tragic flaw"—a built-in weakness in the hero that sabotages any major action he may get going

Following are some examples of internal obstacles from a few great plays:

1. In *Oedipus Rex* by Sophocles, we see the blind arrogance of Oedipus in the very opening speech of the play, in which Oedipus emerges from the central door of his palace and addresses the assembled crowd. It is one of the rare examples of a tragedy beginning with an opening speech by the protagonist:

> Children, young sons and daughters of old Cadmus,
> why do you sit here with your suppliant crowns?
> The town is heavy with a mingled burden

of sounds and smells, of groans and hymns and incense;
I did not think it fit that I should hear
of this from messengers but came myself—
I, Oedipus, whom all men call the Great.[2]

Everything would be perfectly okay if it weren't for that last line
—Oedipus is so sure that *he* is the only one who can unravel the mystery
of the plague that is raging against Thebes. This, of course, is his tragic
flaw of pride which is the internal obstacle that will eventually overcome
Oedipus, in spite of his heroic major action of discovery.

2. In the first act of *Hamlet*, Hamlet himself gives the best description ever
written of the tragic flaw, a built-in weakness that will corrupt anyone
regardless of their other excellences:

So, oft it chances in particular men,
That for some vicious mole of nature in them,
As, in their birth, wherein they are not guilty,
(Since nature cannot choose his origin),
By the o'ergrowth of some complexion,
Oft breaking down the pales and forts of reason,
Or by some habit that too much o'erleavens
The form of plausive manners; that these men,
Carrying, I say, the stamp of one defect,
Being nature's livery, or fortune's star,
Their virtues else, be they as pure as grace,
As infinite as man may undergo,
Shall in the general censure take corruption
From that particular fault . . .[3]

3. Another example of an internal obstacle can be seen in a speech by
Nina in Chekhov's *The Sea Gull*. Nina is talking to Treplev, and she is
having a difficult time thinking clearly, as she keeps coming up against
obstacles inside herself: her resistance to the love of Treplev, the offstage
laughter of her lover Trigorin who has done all he could do to discourage
her acting career, and the haunting image of a sea gull which someone
killed one day out of sheer boredom:

Why did you say you kissed the ground that I walked on? Someone
ought to kill me (*she droops over the table*) I am so tired. Oh, I wish I
could rest . . . just rest! (*she raises her head*) I'm a sea gull . . . No,
that's not it . . . I'm an actress. Oh, well! (*she hears ARKADINA and
TRIGORIN laughing offstage, she listens, then she runs to the door at the left
and she looks through the keyhole*) So he is here too! (*she returns to Treplev*)
Oh, well! Never mind . . . Yes . . . He didn't believe in the theatre.
He was always laughing at my dreams, and so gradually I ceased to
believe too and lost heart . . . And then I was so preoccupied with
love and jealousy and a constant fear for my baby. I became petty and

common. When I acted I did it stupidly. I didn't know what to do with my hands or how to stand on the stage. I couldn't control my voice. But you can't imagine what it feels like—when you know that you are acting abominably. I'm a sea gull. No, that's not it again . . . [4]

In every play, an action comes up against an obstacle and that creates dramatic tension. The stronger the action, the greater the obstacle has to be to resist that action and create strong dramatic tension. The greatest art will always be a combination of massive major actions coming up against insuperable obstacles: Job pitting himself against the wrath of the living God, or King Lear opposing himself to the furious storm on the heath, or Ahab going out against Moby Dick and the scope of the whole wide open ocean. These are epic confrontations, and they consist in a great major action coming up against great obstacles.

Obstacles will always be external or internal, depending on whether the drama is principally outer or inner—though in some cases, a play can contain a combination of both inner and outer obstacles, as in *Hamlet*, where we see the character's major action coming up against both external and internal obstacles.

ADVICE FOR PLAYWRIGHTS

Train yourself to create strong obstacles for every major action in your play.

SUGGESTED READING

Toby Cole: *Playwrights on Playwriting*, Dramabook, 1961.

EXERCISES

1. Write a brief scene with a character who has a strong major action, and then create a strong obstacle for that action.

2. Write a brief scene with a character who has a tragic flaw, so he is his own obstacle to whatever major action he may try to initiate.

3. Write a brief scene with a character who faces a strong external obstacle, and show how this obstacle frustrates any major action he may try to initiate. Decide for yourself whether you want the character to overcome the obstacle eventually.

CHAPTER 5

HOW MUCH IS AT STAKE?

Stakes in a play are crucial.

A playwright may write a play with strong major actions, and he may put in sharp clear visuals that embody those actions, and he may create adequate obstacles to all the actions—yet if the stakes of a play are not appropriate, the whole thing may seem to be vaguely misshapen and off-balance.

What are these "stakes"?

Stakes are how badly the characters in a play want what they say they want, and how appropriate and important this wanting is in view of the total circumstances of the play.

The word "mistake" comes from a miscalculation of stakes. Something is a "mis-stake" if it is a misjudgment of how appropriate or important something actually is.

For example, if the characters in a play don't really care as much as they should about what they say they want, then the audience won't really care all that much about what happens to these characters. If a character says "so what?" then the audience will also say "so what?"

But an audience cannot be allowed to say "so what?" about a play, because that means the audience has lost interest, and that is fatal to playwriting.

The only way to keep an audience's interest in a play is to locate the appropriate stakes for the major actions and circumstances of a play.

Of course an artful inappropriateness of stakes can sometimes be overwhelmingly powerful and moving. Even in low farce, an audience has to believe that the greatest simpleton cares very much about what he says he wants, otherwise the whole thing becomes silly and a waste of our time. It was the comic genius of Charlie Chaplin that he made his sad tramp character seem to care about his action out of all proportion to his circumstances. During the worst calamities, Chaplin was always polite, always tipped his derby to everyone in sight, and always pursued his modest action with a ferocity and a persistence that seemed to be unnatural—which made for uproarious humor. Likewise in high tragedy, sometimes a character will seem to care about his action beyond all reasonable appropriateness, as when King Lear encourages the storm on the heath to make even worse rampages, and assails nature herself for all the injustices done to the tiniest creatures. This seems so heroically inappropriate that it becomes pathetic and heartrending for an audience to witness.

Sometimes the characters in a play will seem to create the stakes of the play through the sheer force of their actions. In *Waiting For Godot* by Samuel Beckett, both Vladimir and Estragon behave onstage as if waiting for Godot were the most important thing in the world. Now *we* may not know why this should be so, or who or what Godot is, or why these two tramps should want to be waiting for Godot —but the fact that Vladimir and Estragon both believe that their entire destiny depends on waiting for Godot, makes us feel that the stakes of the play are overwhelmingly important. However, if either of these tramps began to doubt the importance of waiting for Godot, then we would have a different kind of play on our hands. It would lose its impact on us, and we would begin to wonder why we ourselves were sitting through such a pointless farce of senseless word play and endlessly rambling speeches. In other words, because the stakes of the play had become inappropriate, the play itself would lose all significance.

The same holds true for any play. If no one really cared very much whether Oedipus actually killed his own father and married his mother, then the play *Oedipus Rex* would no longer be much of a tragedy—we'd probably see it as some quaint historical record of someone who just kept making a lot of mistakes.

And in fact both comedy and tragedy can easily be made interchangeable simply by shifting the stakes of the actions and the circumstances. Think of *Hamlet* and *Don Quixote*: For Hamlet, with his major action to kill the reigning monarch of Denmark whom he knows to be a murderer, the stakes are life and death; whereas for Don Quixote, with his major action of tilting at windmills which he believes to be adversaries, the stakes are purely delusional. But we could turn the tables on both of these characters, and make Hamlet ridiculous and Don Quixote tragic, simply by shifting the stakes of their respective situations. Suppose Claudius were completely innocent of any murder and Hamlet had just dreamed up the ghost; and suppose there were real assassins who were hidden away inside all those windmills—now we've shifted the stakes in both of these stories, and consequently the major actions of both characters will be seen in a completely different light.

Stakes, as we said, are crucial; it is vital for a playwright to choose the appropriate stakes for the actions and the circumstances of a play.

Aristotle in the *Poetics* says that all tragedy is the imitation of an action that is serious, complete, and *of a certain magnitude*. It's the "magnitude" that concerns us here—how great the stakes of the action are, how badly the characters want what they say they want. And the stakes of the circumstances will also be crucially important.

How does a playwright go about choosing appropriate stakes for his play?

The best way is to look at the actions and the circumstances of each play, and then exercise a continuous testing of what would happen if the stakes of the play were raised or lowered in any way.

Following are three examples of this process. We can see how the choices of stakes that we make in these examples produce radically different feelings about any play that we might write. Here are the examples:

1. Someone is polishing his shoes. So what? The person could be going to his own wedding, which would make the action of polishing his shoes a

very happy one. Or then again, he could be going to his wife's funeral, which would make the action a very sad one. Or he could be sitting in a jail cell awaiting his own execution, which would make his action a very pathetic one. Or he could just be getting ready to go out for a walk, which would make his action of polishing his shoes just a piece of stage business.

In each of the above instances, the character would approach the action of shining his shoes differently, depending on the different stakes of the dramatic situation. And we ourselves would feel differently about watching the character shining his shoes, depending on what we understood the stakes to be.

2. Someone is lighting a cigarette. So what? It's a casual enough gesture. But if we had just learned this person has lung cancer, his action would be almost unbearable to watch. Suppose we saw this person was sitting on top of a keg of dynamite while he was lighting his cigarette: we would fear for our own safety as well. But suppose we are told the person has just gotten out of bed having made love to someone he cares about very much, then his lighting the cigarette becomes a happy and relaxed event.

3. This book you are reading right now has a cover on it. So what? All books have covers, in order to keep the pages together. And the front covers have decorative designs that help sell the book. But suppose you found out the cover of this book had been treated with dioxide acid, which will cause your hands to drop off in two or three months. Now your feelings about reading the rest of this book will probably change.

Simply by shifting the stakes in each of the above examples, we have produced radically different feelings in the reader. And the same thing can take place in a play, when a playwright shifts the stakes of any dramatic situation. In fact, varying the stakes can be one of the most powerful techniques of playwriting.

Are there any fixed rules or guidelines one can use to determine what the stakes of a play should be, beyond the continuous testing of actions and circumstances?

Well, it would probably be fair to say that the more serious the stakes are, the more serious a play will be. And if the stakes are overwhelmingly powerful, as they are in most tragedies, then the play itself will be correspondingly powerful. Aristotle hints at this in the *Poetics* when he says:

> Whenever the tragic deed, however, is done within the family—when
> murder or the like is done or meditated by brother on brother, by son
> on father, by mother on son, or son on mother—these are the
> situations the playwright should seek after.[1]

This is to say, the playwright should choose actions that take place within the family, because the stakes are always highest there —because incest and parricide and matricide are things that always evoke the strongest feelings in us. And even if one doesn't want to deal with such strongly charged actions, it's still true that most great plays have life and death stakes which involve everyone onstage in tremendous consequences. It is no accident that most Shakespearean tragedies end with the stage piled high with dead bodies, because the stakes have been so fatally high for everyone concerned.

And it's probably also fair to say that the more inappropriate the stakes are, the more comic the play will be. Because in comedy, whatever is incongruous or ludicrous or out of whack strikes us as funny. In *Lysistrata* by Aristophanes, the very serious issue of peace or war is discussed by the women of Athens, but the means they choose to pursue it with is a complete denial of all sex. The Greeks felt these stakes were entirely inappropriate to the situation, so the results were seen as comic and farcical.

Of course it's possible for a playwright to choose appropriate stakes for the actions and circumstances of a play, and the audience to find those stakes inappropriate. Ibsen's *A Doll's House* is a good case in point. At the time that play was produced, audiences were unready to accept the sight of any woman walking out of a bad marriage, no matter how spiritually crippling and soul-stifling it might have been for her to stay. No one wanted to accept the stakes of the play as Ibsen had written it, and in fact some later productions in Scandinavia had Nora pack her bags, leave the house and walk away—only to turn around and go right back up to the door, knock, and ask to be readmitted to the house! That new ending to the play was supposed to mitigate the stakes and show audiences that bad marriages weren't really so insufferable after all.

The same thing happened with Strindberg's play *The Father*, when critics and audiences claimed the stakes were inappropriate because families weren't all that lethal. Strindberg lashed out at his critics and claimed that the stakes of his play were indeed appropriate:

My tragedy *The Father* was recently criticized for being too sad—as if one wants cheerful tragedies! Everybody is clamoring for this supposed "joy of life", and theatre managers demand farces, as if the joy of life consisted in being ridiculous and portraying all human beings as suffering from St. Vitus' Dance or total idiocy. I myself find the joy of life in its strong and cruel struggles, and my pleasure in learning, in adding to my knowledge.[2]

When a playwright chooses the appropriate stakes for a play, as Ibsen and Strindberg did in our modern theatre, and the audience is not ready to accept these stakes, then all one can do is wait for the passage of time to correct an audience's perception. Certainly tinkering around with a play to adapt the stakes to an audience's whim will only ruin the effect of the play and compromise the intentions of the playwright.

As we said at the outset, stakes in a play are crucial. Everything else about a play may be excellent, but if the stakes are inappropriate, the whole thing may seem to be misconceived and ineffective.

ADVICE FOR PLAYWRIGHTS

Train yourself to gauge the appropriate stakes for the major actions of your characters, and for the dramatic circumstances of your plays.

SUGGESTED READING

Antonin Artaud: *The Theatre and its Double,* Grove Press, 1958.

EXERCISES

1. Write a brief scene in which someone is about to jump off a cliff, and choose the stakes so this action will be seen first as tragic, then as comic.

2. Write a brief scene about someone's wanting to get married, and then choose the stakes so this action will be seen first as comic, then as tragic.

3. Write a brief scene where someone sees something as tragic but everyone else sees it as comic, and then reverse the situation so someone sees something as comic but everyone else sees it as tragic.

CHAPTER 6

CHARACTER IS ACTION

In chapter three we said that action is the heart and soul of drama, and we defined action as a character's want, a need, a desire, an objective: what one has to have.

We said every character has to have an action, an objective, something that he wants very much. We said action is what makes every character dramatic, because it is each character's entire reason for being up there onstage.

Now we can go even further, and say that character *is* action.

Hamlet *is* his desire to avenge his murdered father—anything else you may say about him, from a dramatic point of view, is superfluous. Although Hamlet can be described as melancholy or philosophical or poetic, these are merely adjectives open to literary interpretation. What matters is what Hamlet *wants*, what his objective is—which is to say, what Hamlet's *action* is.

Hamlet *is* his action, no more, and no less.

This is a hard thing for some people to accept, especially if they

rained in a literary tradition that sees character as a
.ory for all sorts of qualities and psychological predispositions.
.s recently as the nineteenth century, "character" was seen as a
catch-all for a lot of literary ideas about someone's moral virtues or
someone's aesthetic proclivities or someone's intellectual slant. No
less a novelist than Thomas Hardy in *The Mayor of Casterbridge* quotes
Novalis as saying "Character is Fate"—and though that sounds
pretty impressive, it's hardly dramatic, and it would fall flat onstage.
How many Gothic novels are there about eccentric landowners with
crazy wives locked away in the upstairs bedrooms, in which the
landowners are always interviewing naive governesses to take care of
their innocent offspring? But these are not really "characters" in any
dramatic sense of the word—they're more like caricatures, or
archetypes, or creatures out of some deep sea dream.

As far as drama is concerned, we'll stand by our statement:
character is action. And the stronger the action, the stronger the
character will be.

This may sound simple enough, but how does a playwright go
about locating the major action of a character he is writing?

A playwright may have to go through a long period of living with
his imaginary character, to find out what his major action is. Ibsen
reports this:

> Before I write down one word, I have to have the character in mind
> through and through, and I must penetrate into the last part of his
> soul—the individual comes before anything else—the stage set,
> etc. . . .[1]

This means that in order to locate a character's major action, a
playwright has to go inside himself and uncover some impulse that is
probably hidden away deep in his own unconscious; then he has to
allow this impulse to express itself to the playwright as a conscious
dramatic action. This process is probably the single most difficult and
frustrating and block-creating aspect of playwriting—the search for
the truth of an action which necessitates a descent inside oneself. It
is probably the most important reason why so many playwrights
abandon their plays, or opt for a lot of facile and gimmicky plot lines,
or else do anything they can think of to outwit this arduous
psychological pilgrimage into the forbidden regions inside themselves. Yet we know that without this descent, without this arduous

pilgrimage, there can be no true dramatic writing. Eugene O'Neill writes:

> One's outer life passes in a solitude haunted by the masks of others; one's inner life passes in a solitude hounded by the masks of oneself.[2]

But if one can perservere in this inner search, this exercise in unmasking oneself, one can eventually realize the truth of a major action out of the depths of oneself. And this is the highest experience one can have in playwriting, far beyond any external goals of production or publication or material remuneration. The fact that one has given shape and form to some major action out of oneself, is enough to make up for all the difficulty and frustration and blocks that one has had to endure during the long patient struggle of creation.

Once one has located a character's major action out of oneself, one has to consider how this action fits into a particular dramatic situation. This means the playwright must explore all the specific facts about a character—his age, his race, his sexuality, his social status, his background, his education, his childhood, perhaps even his dream life—no matter how irrelevant these facts may seem to the job at hand. These are called the "given circumstances" of a character, and they can usually be arrived at by answering the following questions:

1. Who am I?

2. What do I want?

3. Where am I right now?

4. Why am I here?

5. When is all this taking place?

6. What is my physical life? What kind of clothes am I wearing? What is in my pockets or my purse, how does my hair look, what am I doing with my hands, what kind of shoes am I wearing, etc?

Once all these questions have been answered, the playwright should then consider the stakes of the dramatic situation—how badly does the character want what he says he wants?

Then the playwright should introduce the other characters in the play with all of their actions, to see how the major character will interact with these other characters and actions. This is where the true dynamics of playwriting comes in, with an easy back and forth exchange among all the characters. Ideally it should happen moment by moment onstage, with all the characters letting their actions happen to them so they are propelled along from beat to beat and from scene to scene.

It's a little like a tennis game, in which one character serves and another returns, the first lobs, the other returns, the first slices, the other returns—and so on, in an easy give and take of dramatic actions that are happening in the play. This means the playwright has to be free and open to this exchange of actions between his characters, and not try to impose any of his own notions or ideas on them.

One way to represent this interplay of actions among the characters is to make a rough sketch diagram of the major action lines of all the characters, to see how each character sends and receives major actions from each of the other characters. One should use the simplest kind of diagram possible, as in figure 6-1:

A ←⟶ B

(Figure 6-1)

This is the simplest kind of two character diagram, where each character is giving and receiving equal actions. If we wanted to show that one character is giving an action and the other character is setting up an obstacle to that action, we would represent it this way (figure 6-2):

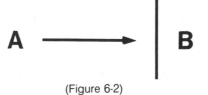

(Figure 6-2)

With three characters, we would use a familiar triangle diagram (figure 6-3):

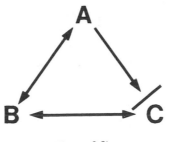

(Figure 6-3)

Here we see the three characters are giving and receiving major actions from each other. Notice that one of the arrowheads, AC, is bolder than the others—this indicates that A's action to C is the major action of the whole scene. And C is setting up an obstacle to that major action. Meanwhile A and B, and B and C, are exchanging action lines from each other in an easy give and take manner.

If there are more characters, one can adjust the diagram accordingly. For example, here is a familiar box diagram (figure 6-4) for four characters, where each character is giving and receiving actions from every other character:

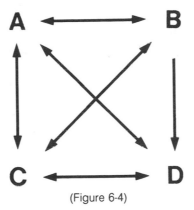

(Figure 6-4)

Once again, remember that all the arrowheads have to be filled in. If one arrowhead is missing, as in D to B above, that's a sign that a major action is missing from the playscript and the playwright had better go back and fill it in somehow in the writing.

There can be other variations on these action diagrams. For example, any character who has a strong action to go somewhere or do something that is outside the immediate onstage situation, could be represented this way (figure 6-5):

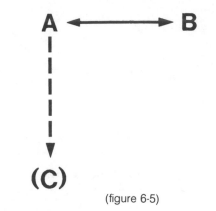

(figure 6-5)

In the above diagram, (C) represents whatever the offstage goal or objective is that A wants to pursue, at the same time that A is exchanging onstage actions with B.

Similarly, it is possible to have an offstage character who exerts a very real influence over one of the onstage characters—for example, a loved one who is far away, who is sending and receiving action lines from one of the onstage characters.

That would be represented this way (figure 6-6):

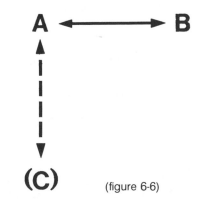

(figure 6-6)

Obviously no one is saying that a playwright could ever write a play just by setting up one of these diagrams and then deriving a plot from it and writing the rest of the play around it. That would be a foolish kind of formulaic thinking that goes against everything we know about the creative process. But these action diagrams do help a playwright keep track of what is happening in his play—they are a kind of shorthand notation system. By using these diagrams, the playwright can see at a glance when there is not an arrowhead leading from one character to another, which is always a sign that there is a missing major action that has to be filled in. Because as we have said, no character can ever be allowed to remain onstage without giving and receiving actions from all the other characters, or setting up an obstacle to the actions.

It's a little like magnets giving off magnetism—the magnetic force will affect all the other magnets that are in the same energy field, and if there's any magnet that is not participating in the back and forth exchange of energies, then there is something wrong with that particular magnet.

Remember what we said in chapter 3 about how no actor is ever going to be caught onstage without having a clear dramatic action which is his whole reason for being there. We can take that a step further now, and say that no actor will ever be caught onstage without both giving and receiving actions from all the other characters who are onstage with him.

And if those clear actions are not immediately evident in a playscript, the actor will make up some actions of his own, to give and receive onstage. And these may very likely be things the playwright did not intend at all, and they might very well upset the logic of the playwright's action diagram. But if that happens, it will be the playwright's own fault, for not having written an "actor-proof" play—which is to say, for not having written clear enough actions for the actor's character to give and receive.

As we said, character *is* action.

ADVICE FOR PLAYWRIGHTS

Train yourself to create characters with strong clear major actions, so the characters can give and receive these actions from each other.

SUGGESTED READING

Friedrich Nietzsche: *The Birth of Tragedy* (any edition).

EXERCISES

1. Write down the given circumstances of a character and answer all the questions about who he is, what he wants, where he is, why he is where he is, when this is all taking place, and what his physical life is like.

2. Write a brief scene with four characters, and then draw an action diagram and trace the action lines from each character to each of the other characters, and indicate the major action of the scene with an extra bold arrowhead.

3. Write a brief scene that has an offstage character who gives and receives as many actions as the onstage characters do.

CHAPTER 7

DIALOGUE AND MOTIFS

Once one has mastered the techniques of visuals and actions and obstacles and stakes and the creation of character, one can then concentrate on other techniques of playwriting such as the uses of dialogue and dramatic motifs.

Dialogue is an important part of dramatic writing, but it is not so easy to define. One can begin by saying what it is *not*. Dialogue is not a lot of talk talk talk or witty chitchat or scintillating word play onstage—that's nothing but deadwood verbiage that weights a play down and makes it literary and talky. Remember that in chapter 2 we said a playwright has to train himself to translate all his verbal narrative impulses into vivid living onstage visuals.

Very well then—what *is* dialogue, and how should one use it effectively in playwriting?

Dialogue is the rapid back and forth exchange that takes place between onstage characters, and good dramatic dialogue always advances the major actions of the play. ✳

Back and forth, giving and taking, sending and receiving—these were the principles we set down for the interplay of dramatic actions, and these same principles hold for good dramatic dialogue also. The best dialogue will always be an authentic exchange, not of information, but of strong inner actions that take the form of language.

And the important question here is whether good dialogue advances some action or whether it is just a lot of flashy talk. If the dialogue advances an action then it is serving a dramatic purpose; but if it is just flashy talk then it is virtuoso writing and has no place in a serious playscript, no matter how clever or impressive that talk may be.

When dialogue is at its most rapid back and forth exchange, it is in the form of alternating lines of dialogue which were originally called "stichomythia" in Greek theatre. This fast stichomythia dialogue can be seen in the following passage from the famous recognition scene of *Electra* by Sophocles, where the dialogue advances the action of Electra's recognition of her long-lost brother Orestes:

ELECTRA:	And where is Orestes buried?
ORESTES:	Nowhere: the living have no grave.
ELECTRA:	What are you saying?
ORESTES:	Nothing that is not true.
ELECTRA:	You mean the man is alive?
ORESTES:	If I myself am alive.
ELECTRA:	What?—are you the same as he?
ORESTES:	Look at our father's ring and see if I speak true.
ELECTRA:	O happy day!
ORESTES:	Happy in every way!
ELECTRA:	Is this your voice?
ORESTES:	No one else's.
ELECTRA:	And do I hold you in my arms?
ORESTES:	As you will hold me always![1]

Here is another rapid back and forth dialogue, from *Hamlet*—it is a sprightly, lightning-like exchange between Hamlet and Ophelia, which advances Hamlet's action of feigned madness so he can mislead the others he knows are eavesdropping on him:

HAMLET:	Lady, shall I lie in your lap?
OPHELIA:	No, my lord.
HAMLET:	I mean, my head upon your lap?
OPHELIA:	Ay, my lord.
HAMLET:	Do you think I meant country matters?

OPHELIA:	I think nothing, my lord.
HAMLET:	That's a fair thought to lie between maids' legs.
OPHELIA:	What is, my lord?
HAMLET:	Nothing.
OPHELIA:	You are merry, my lord.
HAMLET:	Who, I?
OPHELIA:	Ay, my lord.
HAMLET:	Oh God! your only jig-maker. What should a man do, but be merry? For, look you, how cheerfully my mother looks, and my father died within's two hours.[2]

Dialogue does not always have to be in such strict alternating lines—it can also take the form of one person speaking in extended lines to another person, as in the following speech from *The Entertainer* by John Osborne. Phoebe's sudden rhythmic outburst advances her action of scolding poor old Billy Rice who has mistakenly eaten some cake that was on the table:

You've been at that cake.
You've been at my cake.
You've been at my cake, haven't you?
That cake was for Mick.
I bought it for Mick.
It was for when he comes home.
What do you mean—never mind!
Tell him to keep out of it.
It's not much, and it's not mine,
but I mind very much.
Why couldn't you leave it alone?[3]

Aside from these traditional forms of alternating line dialogue and extended line dialogue, there can be very effective use of more sophisticated types of dialogue, such as parallel dialogue and cross dialogue.

Parallel Dialogue. This is where two sets of dialogue are proceeding onstage at the same time, parallel to one another. This usually occurs between two sets of characters, as in *Romeo and Juliet*, where Sampson and Gregory of the Capulets are taunting Abraham and Balthasar of the Montagues. Sampson wants to insult Abraham, which is one level of dialogue, but he also wants to check with Gregory to find out whether he can get away with it, which forms another level of dialogue. And both levels of dialogue take place onstage at the same time:

GREGORY:	I will frown as I pass by, and let them take it as they list.
SAMPSON:	Nay, as they dare. I will bite my thumb at them; which is a disgrace to them, if they bear it.
ABRAHAM:	Do you bite your thumb at us, sir?
SAMPSON:	I do bite my thumb, sir.
ABRAHAM:	Do you bite your thumb at us, sir?
SAMPSON:	(aside to GREGORY) Is the law of our side if I say ay?
GREGORY:	(aside to SAMPSON) No.
SAMPSON:	No, sir, I do not bite my thumb at you, sir; but I bite my thumb, sir.[4]

Another example of parallel dialogue is in *Macbeth*, where a Doctor of Physic and a Waiting Gentlewoman are talking together as they observe Lady Macbeth, who is sleepwalking onstage. Suddenly Lady Macbeth begins to speak, but her dialogue has no relation to anything the Doctor and Gentlewoman are saying. Lady Macbeth is off in her own world with her own dramatic focus, so everything she says is parallel to the other dialogue that is going on:

GENTLEWOMAN:	Lo you! here she comes. This is her very guise; and, upon my life, fast asleep. Observe her; stand close.
DOCTOR:	How came she by that light?
GENTLEWOMAN:	Why, it stood by her: she has light by her continually; 'tis her command.
DOCTOR:	You see, her eyes are open.
GENTLEWOMAN:	Ay, but their sense is shut.
DOCTOR:	What is it she does now? Look, how she rubs her hands.
GENTLEWOMAN:	It is an accustomed action with her, to seem thus washing her hands. I have known her to continue in this a quarter of an hour.
LADY MACBETH:	Yet here's a spot.
DOCTOR:	Hark! she speaks. I will set down what comes from her, to satisfy my remembrance the more strongly.
LADY MACBETH:	Out, damned spot! out, I say! One; two; why, then, 'tis time to do't. Hell is murky! Fie, my lord, fie! a soldier, and afeard? What need we fear who knows it, when none can call our power to account? Yet who would have thought the old man to have had so much blood in him?[5]

Cross Dialogue. This is where two levels of dialogue intercut one another, sometimes in mid-sentence—as in *Hamlet*, where Hamlet is talking with Ophelia about one thing and suddenly switches over to ask her about her father, suspecting that Polonius may be eavesdropping on their scene:

HAMLET:	. . . What should such fellows as I do crawling between earth and heaven? We are arrant knaves, all; believe none of us. Go thy ways to a nunnery. Where's your father?
OPHELIA:	At home, my lord.
HAMLET:	Let the doors be shut upon him, that he may play the fool nowhere but in's own house. Farewell . . .[6]

Monologues should also be considered as a species of dialogue, insofar as good monologues always give and receive strong major actions from some imaginary character focus, in the same way good dialogues give and receive actions from actual onstage characters.

For anyone to stand alone onstage and carry on an unfocused monologue is not only undramatic, it's also unrealistic. Because the truth is we do not usually "talk to ourselves" when we are alone; we are usually talking to some other imaginary person, such as our father or mother or boyfriend or girlfriend or husband or wife or son or daughter, or our boss or our next-door neighbor or someone we just met yesterday. They are not there but we are talking to them nevertheless, and we usually have some very strong action behind what we are saying to them: we want them to know certain things, or we want to show them we aren't afraid of them, or we want to tell them something we forgot to tell them before.

So we are not really "talking to ourselves" at all, nor are we carrying on a "monologue." It is really an imaginary dialogue with a sharp focus on the person who isn't there, and with a strong major action towards that person. And that's the way onstage monologues should be written—as if the other person were actually there, to receive your character's major action, and even occasionally to return that major action.

One of the great "monologues" is when Lady Macbeth comes onstage reading a letter from Macbeth, and then begins "talking" to the imaginary Macbeth, saying all she is thinking about how Macbeth could be king if he would only seize the present opportunity. It is a sort of "dry run" rehearsal for what she will actually say when Macbeth does appear onstage:

Glamis thou art, and Cawdor, and shalt be
What thou art promised. Yet do I fear thy nature;

It is too full 'o the milk of human kindness
To catch the nearest way. Thou wouldst be great;
Art not without ambition, but without
The illness should attend it. What thou wouldst highly,
That wouldst thou holily; wouldst not play false,
And yet wouldst wrongly win . . .[7]

One of the great monologues in the modern theatre is in *The Matchmaker* by Thornton Wilder, when Dolly Levi comes forward to address her dead husband, Ephraim Levi, and tells him of her decision to remarry:

Ephraim Levi, I'm going to get married again. Ephraim, I'm marrying Horace Vandergelder for his money. I'm going to send his money out doing all the things you taught me. Oh, it won't be a marriage in the sense that we had one—but I shall certainly make him happy, and Ephraim—I'm tired. I'm tired of living from hand to mouth, and I'm asking your permission, Ephraim—will you give me away?

(Now addressing the audience, she holds up the purse)

Money! Money!—it's like the sun we walk under; it can kill or cure.—Mr. Vandergelder's money! Vandergelder's never tired of saying most of the people in the world are fools, and in a way he's right, isn't he? Himself, Irene, Cornelius, myself! But there comes a moment in everybody's life when he must decide whether he'll live among human beings or not—a fool among fools or a fool alone. As for me, I've decided to live among them.

I wasn't always so. After my husband's death I retired into myself. Yes, in the evenings, I'd put out the cat, and I'd lock the door, and I'd make myself a little rum toddy; and before I went to bed I'd say a little prayer, thanking God that I was independent—that no one else's life was mixed up with mine. And when ten o'clock sounded from Trinity Church tower, I fell off to sleep and I was a perfectly contented woman. And one night, after two years of this, an oak leaf fell out of my Bible. I had placed it there on the day my husband asked me to marry him; a perfectly good oak leaf—but without color and without life. And suddenly I realized that for a long time I had not shed one tear; nor had I been filled with the wonderful hope that something or other would turn out well. I saw that I was like that oak leaf, and on that night I decided to rejoin the human race.

Yes, we're all fools and we're all in danger of destroying the world with our folly. But the surest way to keep us out of harm is to give us the four or five human pleasures that are our right in the world, —and that takes a little *money!* The difference between a little money and no money at all is enormous—and can shatter the world. And the difference between a little money and an enormous amount of money is very slight—and that, also, can shatter the world.

Money, I've always felt, money—pardon the expression—is like manure; it's not worth a thing unless it's spread about encouraging young things to grow.

Anyway,—that's the opinion of the second Mrs. Vandergelder.[8]

Besides dialogue, another important technique of playwriting is the use of dramatic motifs.

Motifs are the underlying poetic themes of a play, and they usually take the form of verbal metaphors or visual emblems for what the play is all about.

Motifs do not need any special development or resolution, only a clear statement and reiteration in order to establish them as a recurrent mosaic of underlying themes.

In *Who's Afraid of Virginia Woolf?* by Edward Albee, the motifs help to highlight the major actions of the play. The play takes place in a town called New Carthage, which brings to mind the scorched earth sterility of the Punic Wars. And there are other images of sterility that occur throughout the play—the childless George and Martha Washington, castration, vasectomy, geldings, and creatures with broken backs. These motifs of sterility versus fertility all relate to the actions of George and Martha and Nick and Honey in the play itself.

Dramatic motifs can also extend to the naming of characters within the play. Just as medieval plays used allegorical names like Everyman and Death, so in our modern theatre, Arthur Miller's choice of the name Willy Loman expresses the play's motif in the name "Low man." And Tennessee Williams named characters and places to express motifs such as Blanche du Bois (white woods), Stella (for starlight), Belle Reve (beautiful dream), Chance Wayne (Luck running out)—and other names became poetic emblems like Brick, Big Daddy, Boss Finley, Heavenly, and Harry Steed.

A word of warning about dramatic motifs: it does no good to get too intellectual about them, or to try to read too much symbolism into them. They should function as poetic images that arise freely and easily out of the dramatic situation of the play.

Following are some examples of dramatic motifs:

birth versus death
the loss of innocence
appearance versus reality

illusion versus truth
the ravaging of time
good versus evil
corruption versus integrity

Even if a playwright interweaves his motifs skillfully throughout a play and finds verbal metaphors and visual emblems to make them meaningful to an audience, even so, he may still be misunderstood as to their significance. Henrik Ibsen was continually protesting that he was more a poet than a social philosopher—he meant that he cared more for his dramatic motifs than for any underlying issues they may have been seen as illustrating. Thus when a Norwegian Society for Women's Rights gave Ibsen a testimonial dinner, he said:

> I thank you for your toast but I must decline the honor of consciously having worked for women's rights. I am not even quite sure what women's rights really are. To me it has been a question of human rights.[9]

And in 1939, Tennessee Williams wrote to his agent, Audrey Wood:

> As you have observed by now, I have only one major theme for all my work which is the destructive impact of society on the sensitive, non-conformist individual.[10]

Dramatic motifs, like dialogue, are important techniques of playwriting and can help to complete the sense of a play's being an organic, living whole.

ADVICE FOR PLAYWRIGHTS

Train yourself to make effective use of dialogue and dramatic motifs in playwriting.

SUGGESTED READING

Jean-Louis Barrault: *The Theatre of Jean-Louis Barrault,* Theatre Arts, 1946.

EXERCISES

1. Write a dialogue in which two characters argue about something, while two other characters eavesdrop and comment on the argument.

2. Write a monologue in which a character talks to an imaginary person about something the character cares about very much.

3. Make a list of dramatic motifs for a play, and then make up a cast list of character names that will reflect these motifs.

CHAPTER 8

EXPOSITION AND TITLES

A telephone rings, or a telegram arrives, or someone reads a newspaper article out loud, or a carrier pigeon flies onstage and someone opens a secret message that is tied to its leg—these are all cliché ways of providing background information to an audience at the beginning of a play, so the audience will know what the play is going to be all about.

Thornton Wilder wrote a classic spoof of these obvious expositional devices in his play *The Skin of Our Teeth*. The curtain goes up, a maid comes onstage, she sighs, and then begins talking to no one in particular:

Oh, oh, oh! Six o'clock and the master not home yet.

Pray God nothing serious has happened to him crossing the Hudson River. If anything happened to him, we would certainly be inconsolable and have to move into a less desirable residence district . . . [1]

75

The maid goes on and on, talking about Mr. Antrobus, about Mrs. Antrobus, about the children, about the weather, about the state of the universe—and then, as if to rub our nose in how hopelessly stupid this kind of exposition is, the maid goes back and begins to repeat the same opening lines of the play once again.

The problem of exposition: How do you get across the necessary background material that an audience needs to know about a play, without seeming to "telegraph" a lot of information in a heavy-handed and obvious way?

Before we answer that question, we'd better be clear as to what exposition really is.

Exposition—the word comes from its roots "ex" and "posit," and it means literally "out of the place." In other words, where something is coming from. Exposition should provide necessary background material for the play concerning where things are taking place. Specifically, exposition will relate to what is taking place onstage in the following three areas:

1. *Prior actions:* What actions were happening just prior to the play's beginning?

2. *Offstage actions:* What actions are taking place offstage during the course of the play?

3. *Given circumstances:* What conditions may be affecting the physical life of the characters that are onstage?

A playwright must find ways of presenting this exposition so an audience will not feel it is being imposed on by a lot of "information." Because who wants to sit through an interminable parade of facts and figures, just so one will know what is going on?

Well, we're not so sure. The problem may not have anything to do with presenting a lot of facts and figures because, if it's done in the right way, an audience will usually get a great deal of pleasure out of learning anything. We remember in the *Iliad* how Homer takes time out to recite an endless list of names of all the ships that embarked for the Trojan War. And in the Old Testament, there are all those long genealogies of how so-and-so begat so-and-so. Obviously, ancient audiences got a great deal of pleasure out of informational catalogue listings, and if it's done in the right way, we could probably get the same pleasure out of them also.

The problem is not presenting a lot of information to an audience —the problem is in the *placement* of this material, finding the right place in the play where one can get away with it.

Obviously if one puts all that exposition at the very beginning of the play, as Thornton Wilder did mockingly in *The Skin Of Our Teeth,* an audience will resent it as superfluous information. Because at the beginning of a play, an audience wants to get into the major actions as quickly as possible. Remember that Aristotle tells us that in dramatic writing one should not begin at the beginning, one should begin at the middle—one should thrust an audience into the middle of a major action right away, and then one can always work backwards and fill in the necessary background material at one's leisure.

This is an excellent principle for beginning a play: begin with a bang, the way Olson and Johnson did with *Hellzapoppin* back in 1940. The curtain went up and the facade of a steam engine went hurtling out over the first twenty rows, complete with sound effects and hissing steam to frighten the daylights out of the audience! That was a highly theatrical and comic device, but it certainly illustrates our point about beginning with a bang.

And this principle of a strong opening is used in some of the greatest plays ever written. In *Oedipus Rex,* for example, there is no exposition at all in the beginning—we just see Oedipus walk out onstage and begin telling everyone what a great king he is, and that he is the only one who can discover the cause of the plague in Thebes. In other words, we are thrown right into the midst of a major action before we realize what has hit us.

Similarly, at the beginning of *Macbeth,* three witches come racing onstage and begin cackling about how they are going to meet with Macbeth, and then they run off again. We have no idea what is going on in this play, but we certainly want to know more! And we do learn more, in the very next scene, when the Bloody Sergeant delivers a long expositional speech to King Duncan reporting the progress of the day's battle and how Macbeth overcame both the traitor Macdonwald and the whole Norwegian army.

In the opening scene of *Hamlet* there is a ghost which appears to the sentries on the tower. Talk about beginning with a bang! Then this ghost goes away, so the guards have a chance to sit down in amazement, and—as if to quiet down the guards and assure them that everything is all right—Horatio begins an extraordinarily long expositional speech of 140 lines about the present state of Denmark, the prior events of the late King Hamlet's combat with Fortinbras of Norway, the offstage action of the military buildup of Denmark under Claudius, and the given circumstances of the situation at Elsinore. Horatio even goes into a long comparison with Julius Caesar's Rome, when—suddenly the ghost appears again! This is an excellent example of how one can get away with a tremendous amount of necessary background material, provided one knows how to begin the play powerfully, and where to place the exposition skillfully.

The best way of approaching the problem of exposition is not to see it as so much "information" that has to be passed on to an audience, but to see it as a way of introducing the major actions of the play as quickly as possible—with specific reference to those three areas we mentioned: prior actions, offstage actions, and given circumstances.

Shakespeare's *Tempest* is a good case in point. The play begins with one of the most calamitous scenes ever put onstage: a ship at sea is caught in a tempest and is about to split in half, and everyone on deck is running about in pandemonium. There is one stage direction that is a masterpiece of understatement—"Enter Mariners, wet." By the end of this short opening scene, everyone onstage is aware that the ship is sinking and all is lost.

The very next scene of *The Tempest* is one of the longest scenes in all Shakespeare. Act I, Scene ii, runs about 498 lines, and is principally made up of Prospero telling his daughter Miranda the truth about who he really is:

PROSPERO: . . . What seest thou else
                  In the dark backward and abysm of time?
                  If thou remember'st aught ere thou cam'st here,
                  How thou cam'st here, thou may'st.
MIRANDA: But that I do not.
PROSPERO: Twelve year since, Miranda, twelve year since,
                  Thy father was the Duke of Milan and
                  A prince of power . . . [2]

Prospero proceeds to tell Miranda how he lost the dukedom of Milan through the intrigue of his brother Antonio, and how Prospero was cast adrift at sea with his three year old daughter Miranda, and how they eventually landed on this desert island; the story is so long and complex that Prospero has to keep nudging Miranda to stay awake and pay attention to it.

On the surface of it, this looks like the worst kind of expository writing, because it is so verbal and repetitious and endlessly talky. Most productions try to tighten the scene, or else they flounder through it as if it were nothing but a lot of "information" which an audience has to be spoon-fed for its own good. Whereas, in fact, it is no such thing.

First of all, Shakespeare knows he has the full attention of his audience, having just dazzled them with the short opening ship-wreck scene which is one of the most theatrical scenes ever written. So now he can afford to be leisurely in this great long second scene, and casually unfold the necessary background material of the play. The principle is sound—after watching an automobile accident, an audience would probably pay attention if someone read from the phone book.

Secondly, this long scene is not just a lot of "information" because it introduces Prospero's major action, which happens to be the major action of the play itself: Prospero's obsessive wish to reclaim his rightful dukedom. And that explains why there are so many long speeches in this second scene, because Prospero's major action happens to express itself verbally and even repetitiously, the way all obsessional people keep going over and over the same material endlessly (like the Ancient Mariner, who has to talk and talk and talk about what happened to that damned albatross). But talking itself can be an action, if it is played correctly.

Of course, expositional background material does not *have* to be verbal. The opening scene of *A Streetcar Named Desire* by Tennessee Williams contains an excellent visual expositional device. Stanley Kowalski comes onstage, carrying his bowling jacket and a red-stained package from the butcher shop. He bellows for Stella, who comes out on the first floor landing, and Stanley tosses the package of meat across the stage to her. She catches it. It is like a cave man bringing home the meat from his latest kill, and we sense the major action of the play will have something of that same crude aboriginal ruthlessness.

Following are three other examples of exposition, from three great plays:

1. In *Henry V*, Act I, Scene ii, Henry asks the Archbishop of Canterbury whether he has any right to lay claim on certain lands in France:

> HENRY: My learned lord, we pray you to proceed
>   And justly and religiously unfold
>   Why the Law Salique that they have in France
>   Or should, or should not, bar us in our claim . . . [3]

And the Archbishop does proceed, in lines 33–95, to give an overlong account of Henry's absolute right to claim certain lands in France. The Archbishop's speech covers the history of the Law of Salique as it derives from Charles the Great, the Saxons, the Kings Pharamond, Childeric, Pepin, Blithild, Clothair, Hugh Capet, Charles Duke of Lorraine, Lewis the Tenth, and Queen Isabel. Why on earth, we wonder, does the Archbishop go on and on in such an endless recitation of history?

But this speech is crucial in establishing the stakes of the play: Henry is the ideal Christian monarch and would not invade France unless he were absolutely sure he was on the side of God's Law, so he must explore the legal and historical precedents before making up his mind. Even so, Henry does not decide to wage war until after the French ambassadors enter and insult him with his youth and inexperience. Henry answers by declaring war on France—but by this time we know Henry is not being hot-headed and impetuous, because we have seen him exhaustively exploring all the justifications for this war.

2. In *Our Town* by Thornton Wilder, the Stage Manager gives the following exposition at the beginning of the play:

> This play is called *Our Town*. It was written by Thornton Wilder; produced and directed by A. . . . (or: produced by A . . . ; directed by B . . .). In it you will see Miss C . . . ; Miss D . . . ; Miss E . . . ; and Mr. F . . . ; Mr. G . . . ; Mr. H . . . ; and many others. The name of the town is Grover's Corners, New Hampshire—just across the Massachusetts line: latitude 42 degrees 40 minutes; longitude 70 degrees 37 minutes. The first act shows a day in our town. The day is May 7, 1901. The time is just before dawn. [4]

This has to be one of the most deliberately expositional speeches ever written—what other play do you know that tells the latitude and longitude of where it all takes place?

Thornton Wilder was doing this quite consciously, because he was after a highly stylized kind of theatre. He wanted to write a play that would break "fourth wall" naturalism with its "box-set" stage, which he associated with too many "soothing" middle class plays. He wanted to shake free of too narrow conventions of time and place in a play, so he could focus our attention on the more universal truths of birth and life and marriage and death. And he felt the best way of doing this was to present his exposition in as bald a form as possible, as it is shown above. That way, we would be free to concentrate on the expressive actions that were taking place onstage, and not worry overmuch about specific circumstances of time and place of the play.

This looks like a radical experiment in playwriting but Wilder must have known what he was doing in gauging the problem of exposition for this particular kind of play, because *Our Town* is one of the most performed plays of our time.

3. In *Who's Afraid of Virginia Woolf?* by Edward Albee, the play begins with a bang—George and Martha come onstage, clattering, cursing, with a barrage of verbal abuse:

MARTHA: Jesus . . .
GEORGE: . . . Shhhhhh . . .
MARTHA: . . . H. Christ . . .
GEORGE: For God's sake, Martha, it's two o'clock in the . . .
MARTHA: Oh, George!
GEORGE: Well I'm *sorry* but . . .
MARTHA: What a cluck! What a cluck you are.
GEORGE: It's late, you know? Late.
MARTHA: *(Looks about the room. Imitates Bette Davis)* What a dump. Hey, what's that from? "What a dump!"
GEORGE: How would I know what . . .
MARTHA: Aw, come on! What's it from? *You* know . . .
GEORGE: . . . Martha . . .
MARTHA: WHAT'S IT FROM, FOR CHRIST'S SAKE?[5]

After such a loud, theatrical entrance, we certainly want to know more about what is going on. And actually these few lines have already propelled us quite a way into the major actions of the play—Martha is berating her husband, berating her place, shouting out questions and commands, and George seems to be helpless to placate her.

Seems to be.

Thanks to this excellent opening exposition, we are well on our way into the actions of the play.

Just as exposition can be a way of introducing the major actions of a play, so play titles will usually reveal whether a play is dominated by a major character action or whether a play is more illustrative of some theme or some dramatic motif.

Plays with titles of principal characters will usually be concerned with some major character action, such as the following:

Oedipus Rex	*Saint Joan*
Agamemnon	*The Great God Brown*
Yerma	*Hamlet*
Macbeth	*King Lear*
Othello	*Hedda Gabler*
Uncle Vanya	*Brand*
Miss Julie	*Cyrano de Bergerac*
Major Barbara	*The Emperor Jones*
Galileo	*Mother Courage*

On the other hand, plays with themes or dramatic motifs in the titles will usually be concerned with some central idea of image or dramatic metaphor, such as the following:

The Trojan Women	*The Tempest*
Measure for Measure	*A Midsummer Night's Dream*
The Sea Gull	*The Cherry Orchard*
The Glass Menagerie	*A Streetcar Named Desire*
Death of a Salesman	*A Doll's House*
The Power of Darkness	*The Importance of Being Earnest*
The Dance of Death	*The Lower Depths*
Blood Wedding	*The Threepenny Opera*
Murder in the Cathedral	*The Time of Your Life*
The Skin of Our Teeth	*The Connection*

In fact it is interesting to see how the choice of a title can sometimes reveal the different transitional phases of playwriting. Sometimes a playwright will choose what looks like a throw-away title for his work, such as Shakespeare's *As You Like It;* sometimes playwrights will go through various working titles before they finally decide on the titles we know their work by.

It's interesting to compare the working titles of these plays with the final choices, to see what subtle shifts of emphasis may have taken place as the play began to take on its final form.

Following are some examples of working titles and the final choices:

TABLE 8-1

Playwright	Working title	Final title
Shakespeare	*What You Will*	*Twelfth Night*
Congreve	*The World Well Lost*	*All For Love*
Arthur Miller	*The Inside of His Head*	*Death of a Salesman*

TABLE 8-1

Playwright	Working title	Final title
Tennessee Williams	The Gentleman Caller	The Glass Menagerie
	Portrait of a Girl in Glass	The Glass Menagerie
	Blanche's Chair in the Moon	A Streetcar Named Desire
	The Poker Night	A Streetcar Named Desire
	A Chart of Anatomy	Summer and Smoke
	Orpheus Descending	The Fugitive Kind (film)
	The Milk Train Doesn't Stop Here Anymore	Boom (film)
Thornton Wilder	The Merchant of Yonkers	The Matchmaker
Edward Albee	The Exorcism	Who's Afraid of Virginia Woolf?

ADVICE FOR PLAYWRIGHTS

Train yourself to use exposition and titles to introduce and highlight the major actions of a play.

SUGGESTED READING

John Gassner: *Masters of the Drama*, Random House, 1954.

EXERCISES

1. Write three pages of an opening scene of a play, introducing the major action of a complete play.

2. Write exposition for a play, giving necessary background material for the following three areas: prior actions, offstage actions, and given circumstances.

3. Create five working titles for the same play you might write using the exposition from the previous exercise.

CHAPTER 9

PLOTS AND CONFLICTS

Plots and conflicts are the architecture of playwriting.

It's easy enough to say what plots and conflicts are not. They are not easy formulas or shortcuts to writing a "well made play," what the French call a "pièce bien faite." One French playwright, Scribe, wrote over 500 of these things, and they were all so meticulously plotted that they were hopelessly contrived and mechanical and lifeless. It took Henrik Ibsen to break the mold of these "well made plays" and allow his plays to create their own plots and conflicts out of the major actions of the characters.

George Bernard Shaw gives the formula for the "well made play" in his Preface to *Three Plays* by the French playwright Brieux:

> First you have an idea for a dramatic situation, maybe you manufacture a misunderstanding, someone is wrongfully accused of something —then you plan it out over the course of the play: the first act you introduce the character; the second act you bring the misunderstanding to a head; the third act you clear up the misunderstanding.[1]

This is pretty wretched stuff, and as Shaw himself comments, "No writer of the first order needs the formula any more than a sound man needs a crutch."

And the same holds true for ready-made plots. Astonishing as it sounds, an Italian playwright and critic named Gozzi said there could be no more than thirty-six basic plots—and one of Gozzi's followers, Georges Polti, wrote a book titled *The Thirty-Six Dramatic Situations,* listing what these basic plots were. They were all dramatic premises, and they included such rote formulas as:

"Life sacrificed for the happiness of a relative or a loved one."

"A woman enamored of her stepson."

"Witnessing the slaying of a kinsman, while powerless to prevent it."

One wonders what kind of geometrical mind could waste its time trying to categorize such things, let alone advocate such a silly approach to serious playwriting students.

Because the fact is that whenever plot precedes the major actions of the characters in a play, the result will usually be melodrama and a kind of formula playwriting.

On the other hand, the playwright should be aware of the dangers of plotlessness. Aristotle describes this kind of playwriting:

> Of simple plots and actions the episodic are the worst—I call a plot episodic when there is neither probability nor necessity in the sequence of its episodes.[2]

An episodic plot will meander from scene to scene, will have no strong subtextual major action, and will be both improbable (it couldn't really happen) and not necessary (it doesn't really follow).

Ironically, in our culture today, episodic plots abound on television soap operas. Because on the typical television soap, there are very few onstage *actions;* instead there is mostly just a lot of endless talk talk talk about offstage *situations,* by characters who don't have any major actions apart from their own talking.

The depressing thing about these soaps is that they are so popular—or perhaps "popular" isn't the right word, maybe "addictive" comes closer to the truth. In fact these soaps are so addictive, their "plot" summaries are often published in the daily papers so that if someone misses a favorite daytime soap, he can always find out what "happened." Here are some typical "plot" summaries for a series of typical soaps, taken from a New York newspaper of a few years ago:

All My Children: Erica returned from a tacky hideout to learn that Lars was auditioning a new model. Jenny didn't tell Jesse she's modeling lingerie.

As the World Turns: Ariel cringed when John mentioned he wanted kids. Maggie realized Betsy planned a mountain cabin tryst with Steve.

Capital: A devastated Julie secretly witnessed Tyler in a clinch with Sloane. Lawrence panicked when Kelly accepted a date with Trye.

Days of Our Lives: Trish agreed Scotty could spend the summer with David. Roman was suspicious of Anna's story of being forced into white slavery.

Edge of Night: Calvin was suspended for roughing up Tony, who was arrested for carrying a gun sans permit. Loomis schemed to kill Damien.

One Life To Live: Pat said she'd marry Tony and agreed Jimmy can't live with them while Georgina is in California. Cassie refused to sleep with Gary.

Guiding Light: Kelly sped home from St. Croix after finding Morgan's birth control pills. Quint searched London for Silas who has Nola hidden.

Ryan's Hope: Johnny was miffed that Maeve practiced for a dance contest with David Newman. Kim was dazzled by Amanda but jealous of her.[3]

One can see how few real actions there are in these plot summaries, and how many expository *offstage situations* are being talked about, and how many incongruous juxtapositions of unrelated incidents there are. As Aristotle says, there is not any probability or necessity to the sequence of these episodes.

Then what is the proper approach to plotting?

On the one hand, one does not want to impose a formula or ready-made plot on a play from the outside, because that will result in melodrama and will usually stifle the life of the characters and render them hopelessly literary and stilted. But on the other hand, one cannot allow an episodic plot to go meandering aimlessly from scene to scene with no strong subtextual major action and nothing but a lot of offstage situations that are endlessly talked about.

It's simple enough to see what the proper approach to plotting ought to be, if we remember what we said about plot as the architecture of the major actions of a play. Plot will describe how these major actions proceed over the whole course of an entire play—what turns and reversals and climaxes and denouements the major actions will experience.

But there can be no strict formulas for this plotting, and we cannot say with any certainty what plotting should be in any particular play. True plots will always arise naturally out of the interplay of the major actions of the characters in a play.

The most we can do here is set down a few simple guidelines on how to master the basic techniques of plotting. Following are five of the most useful guidelines:

1. *Audience Knowledge:* The skillful choice of how much an audience does or does not know about what is taking place onstage can add immeasurably to the unfolding of a plot line. For example, in *Electra* by Sophocles, the audience knows the ashes that Electra is holding in the urn are not really those of Orestes, and the audience also knows that the shepherd who has come onstage to sit next to Electra is really Orestes in disguise—so the audience is in an excellent position to anticipate Electra's discovery of Orestes. One can imagine that if the situation were reversed—if the audience knew nothing of who Orestes really was, and if Electra knew everything—then the scene would lose all its power and force. By the same token, the fact that an audience does *not* know who the real killer is in the typical "whodunit" mystery creates the whole pleasure of unraveling the plot line.

2. *Parallel Plotting:* Parallel subplot actions can contrast with major actions in a play, so these major actions are underscored and thrown into relief. For example, in *The Night of the Iguana* by Tennessee Williams, Reverend Shannon is not the only character in the play whose action is to survive an entire night of being at the end of his rope—there is a live iguana onstage that has also been caught, and almost all the other characters in the play are also sharing in the same action of being at the end of their rope. So these other subplot actions reinforce and highlight Shannon's strong major action in the play.

3. *Reversals:* Reversals occur when a major action is going in one direction and suddenly it shifts and begins going in another direction. Reversals are also called "peripeteias" or "turnings." For example, in *Summer and Smoke* by Tennessee Williams, the major character actions of John and Alma reverse halfway through the play. At the beginning of the play, John is hot-blooded and lusty and Alma is chaste and repressed; after the reversal in the play takes place, John settles down as a doctor and becomes staid and proper and Alma becomes hot-blooded and promiscuous. It is an excellent example of a double reversal of major actions.

4. *Climax:* Climax is the peak of intensity of an action, sometimes occasioning a reversal or a discovery action. In other words, the climax can sometimes be a turning point for the whole play. For example, in *Hamlet,* the play within the play scene re-enacts the killing of Hamlet's father with such accuracy that Claudius rises and leaves the court for his own chamber, and Hamlet knows that he has confronted Claudius with his own guilt and all that remains to be done is to avenge him for the murder. We could say, then, that the play within the play is the climax of *Hamlet,* in that it initiates a discovery and is the turning point for the whole play.

5. *Denouement:* Denouement is the final unraveling of a plot. In Greek plays this was usually done with a messenger speech which revealed the final outcome of the tragic action. A modern example is the play *Mister Roberts* by Thomas Heggen and Joshua Logan, where the denouement is made doubly effective through the use of two letters which Ensign Pulver reads. One letter is from Mister Roberts, describing his happiness at finally being in combat—and the second letter is an official announcement of the death of Mister Roberts. This double denouement gives added power to the unraveling of the plot of the play.

As we said, once a playwright has mastered these simple guidelines for the basic techniques of plotting, he will have to discover his own way of shaping the plots of his plays. There can be no strict formulas or ready-made answers to how he should use audience knowledge, parallel plotting, reversals, climax, and denouement in his individual plays. The most important thing is to remain open and intuitive and see where his major actions will lead him, and where and how these plot guidelines will seem to be most appropriate.

Arthur Miller speaks of this need to remain open and intuitive in the writing of his own plays:

> For myself, it has never been possible to generate the energy to write and complete a play if I know in advance everything it signifies and all it will contain. The very impulse to write, I think, springs from an inner chaos crying for order, for meaning, and that meaning must be discovered in the process of writing or the work lies dead as it is finished.[4]

This means that once a playwright has discovered what it is that he wants to write, the best plotting will almost always take place in the subtext of a play, so an audience will not be aware of any conscious patterning or manipulation of the plot as it unfolds up there onstage.

Following are some examples of plot lines that take place in the *subtext* of three great plays, which illustrate some of the guidelines we have just set down:

1. In Racine's *Phèdre,* Phèdre's seduction of her stepson Hippolyte fails, and so she reverses her major action and accuses Hippolyte of trying to seduce her—and Hippolyte's father Theseus calls down the wrath of Neptune on Hippolyte to destroy him.

2. In Ibsen's *Ghosts,* the action of the play concerns "ghosts" and echoes of the bloodstream that keep coming back to haunt us in the form of parallel subplot actions: Oswald begins to repeat the behavior of his father, and the mother realizes she is helpless to break free of the life lies that keep recurring in the form of repetitive situations and, specifically, hereditary syphilis.

3. In Pinter's *The Homecoming,* a dutiful son returns home with his new wife and surrenders her up to his voracious working class family, and in the climax of the play the father begins crawling and groping towards the young woman in a paroxysm of greed and sexual appetite.

As we said at the outset, plots and conflicts are the architecture of playwriting—and as with any architectural creation, the best work is always achieved not through the use of any artificially imposed external form, but when the true shape and form of the whole arises organically from the true nature of the materials.

ADVICE FOR PLAYWRIGHTS

Train yourself to create plot lines that derive naturally from the major actions of the characters in your plays.

SUGGESTED READING

Francis Fergusson: *The Idea of a Theatre,* Princeton, 1949.

EXERCISES

1. Write a brief scene with a major character action, then create some parallel subplot actions to contrast with this major action and throw it into relief.

2. Write a brief scene with a major character action, then create a reversal or turning of this action away from its original objective.

3. Write a brief scene with a major character action, but try to withhold the audience's knowledge of what this major action is.

CHAPTER 10

THE PLAY TEXT ITSELF

Unlike a novel, a playscript is like a musical score—the text does not exist for its own sake alone, but for the sake of what can be done with it by a group of dedicated interpreters who will bring it to life onstage.

As such, it will be to a playwright's advantage to set down his play on the page in accordance with certain uniformities of format that have become conventions in the modern theatre.

First of all, the playwright will have to make certain fundamental decisions about his play. For example, he needs to decide how many acts or scenes his play will have.

Greek plays began as long one-act plays with continuous actions that happened in one time and one place. This gave rise to the three classical unities of time, place, and action, which characterize all the Greek tragedies. But the Roman playwright Seneca noticed that while all the Greek plays were one uninterrupted action, they could nonetheless all be subdivided into five reasonably equal beats or

91

"acts"—and so Seneca divided his plays *Medea* and *Phaedra* and *Oedipus* into five separate acts, and that is where the practice of act division began. By the time Shakespeare began writing his plays in the Renaissance, it was natural for him to break every play into five equal acts, with separate scenes as subdivisions of each act.

This practice continued through the Renaissance, but then playwrights began separating their plays into arbitrary units of their own choice. The result was an extraordinary variety of possibilities in act and scene divisions in plays, and following is a random sampling of the act and scene divisions of certain outstanding modern plays:

TABLE 10-1

Playwright	Play	Division
Molière	*Le Misanthrope*	5 acts
	Tartuffe	5 acts
	The Imaginary Invalid	3 acts
Ibsen	*Peer Gynt*	5 acts
	A Doll's House	3 acts
	Ghosts	3 acts
	The Wild Duck	5 acts
	Hedda Gabler	4 acts
Chekhov	*The Sea Gull*	5 acts
	Uncle Vanya	4 acts
	The Three Sisters	4 acts
	The Cherry Orchard	4 acts
Shaw	*Man and Superman*	4 acts + *Don Juan*
	The Devil's Disciple	3 acts
	Pygmalion	5 acts
	Saint Joan	6 scenes + epilogue
O'Neill	*A Moon For the Misbegotten*	4 acts
	Mourning Becomes Electra	3 parts, 13 acts
	Strange Interlude	9 acts

TABLE 10-1

Playwright	Play	Division
	A Touch of the Poet	4 acts
	Long Day's Journey Into Night	4 acts
Williams	*The Glass Menagerie*	7 scenes
	A Streetcar Named Desire	11 scenes
	Cat on a Hot Tin Roof	3 acts
	Sweet Bird of Youth	3 acts
	The Night of the Iguana	3 acts
	Summer and Smoke	12 scenes
Miller	*Death of a Salesman*	2 acts + requiem
	All My Sons	3 acts
	The Crucible	4 acts
	A View From the Bridge	2 acts
	After the Fall	2 acts
Pinter	*The Caretaker*	2 acts
	The Homecoming	2 acts
Albee	*Who's Afraid of Virginia Woolf?*	3 acts
	The Zoo Story	1 act
Beckett	*Waiting For Godot*	2 acts
	Krapp's Last Tape	1 act
	Endgame	1 act

The variety of act and scene divisions represented in the above list means that in the modern theatre, there are no strict rules for how long a play ought to be, or what the act or scene divisions should be. In view of this, we'd say a playwright had better let his play tell him how many scenes or acts it wants to be, based on a sense of how the major actions of the play choose to evolve. Any other formula or rule seems foolish in light of modern theatre history—although we will point out that in our commercial theatre, there are usually such overwhelming production costs, that one tends to favor the two act play form. Because of that, no matter what the playwright may have chosen for his play form, the decision of where and how many intermissions there may be in any given performance of a play, will invariably be left in the hands of the theatre management and not with the playwright.

Notwithstanding that, a playwright will still need to decide how many scenes and acts his play should have. And his next problem will be how the playscript should be set down in a uniform format that will be acceptable to producers and agents and directors and actors and play publishers.

Following are the generally accepted guidelines for the modern playscript format:

1. Stage directions should be in parentheses and underlined for italics, and should extend from the left hand margin all the way across to the right hand margin.

2. All onstage dialogue should be set down with the character's name in capitals and centered in the middle of the page, with any character stage directions on how the lines should be said put in italics immediately under the character's name, with the dialogue itself dropped a double space and indented on both the left and right sides of the page.

Here is the opening scene of *Macbeth* set down in this modern playscript format. We have inserted certain of our own character stage directions that are not in the original Shakespeare text, to show their appropriate placement on the playscript page:

SCENE ONE

(A desert heath. Slabs of rock and broken garbage bags all over the stage. Thunder and lightning, then THREE WITCHES come racing onstage USL and they run across to DSR. They are dressed in pile-on skirts with holes and tatters.)

FIRST WITCH

(helpless)

When shall we three meet again
In thunder, lightning, or in rain?

SECOND WITCH

(commanding)

When the hurlyburly's done,
When the battle's lost and won.

THIRD WITCH

(getting her two cents in)

That will be ere the set of sun.

FIRST WITCH

(still helpless)

Where the place?

SECOND WITCH

(still commanding)

Upon the heath.

THIRD WITCH

(still getting her two cents in)

There to meet with Macbeth.

FIRST WITCH

(suddenly hearing something DSL)

I come, Graymalkin!

SECOND WITCH

(also hearing something DSL)

Paddock calls.

TIIIRD WITCH

(fresh out of small change)

Anon.

ALL

(chanting)

Fair is foul and foul is fair:
Hover through the fog and filthy air.

(They all exit DSR)

This is the standard playscript format that most professional playwrights will use in setting down their characters, dialogue, and stage directions.

How long will a playscript in this standard format take to play, when it is performed onstage? To get some gauge of timing: This *Macbeth* scene has very short lines, and is part of the intention of the scene that it be played extremely quickly. The average play scene that is written in this standard format will take about one minute per page to read out loud, and it will take about a minute and a half per page to play on stage in full performance. Therefore, sixty pages of a playscript in the above format will take about an hour to read out loud, and it will take about an hour and a half to play onstage.

Once one has mastered this standard playscript format, one must still be aware of certain technical problems in setting down one's play in playscript form. Following are the most common difficulties:

1. It's always important with large casts to keep track of all the character entrances and exits so there will be no awkward traffic jams onstage, and it's especially important not to leave anyone onstage who was supposed to leave.

2. One should be very aware of "dead beats," which are spaces or gaps in a playscript where nothing is really happening onstage. For example, a stage direction may read: *(Suzy goes offstage and fries an egg).* This action of frying an egg would take about three minutes to perform, and meanwhile an audience would be sitting on its hands waiting for some major action to begin.

3. For split stage effects with different levels, a playwright must specify the particular areas of the stage for each scene, especially as it will affect any entrances or exits that may be made. Stage directions should be indicated for each and every scene, according to the following stage designations (see figure 10-1):

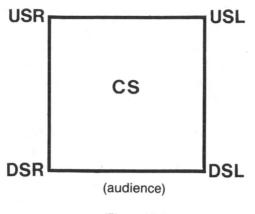

(Figure 10-1)

The abbreviations for the above diagram refer to the following:

CS—center stage
USR—upstage right, towards the rear of the stage
DSR—downstage right, towards the front of the stage
USL—upstage left, towards the rear of the stage
DSL—downstage left, towards the front of the stage

In some eastern European theatres like the Berliner Ensemble and the Moscow Art Theatre, "stage right" and "stage left" will refer to the audience's point of view. But in any play that is to be written and staged in America and England and western Europe, "stage right" and "stage left" will always refer to the actor's right and left as he is standing on stage and facing the audience.

As we said at the outset of this chapter, a playscript is like a musical score. The text exists not for its own sake but for the sake of what can be done with it by a group of dedicated interpreters who will bring it to life onstage. This being the case, it is the playwright's responsibility to try and set down the best possible rough working draft to indicate what that onstage life of the play should be. As Tennessee Williams once said, "Plays do not exist until they are on stage."

Therefore it's important for the playwright to learn as much as possible about the full resources of the stage. Some playwrights will even construct model stages and place stick figures on it to represent their major characters, to get some feel of what the onstage life of a scene will look like. Other playwrights will get up on a real stage and try acting in plays—it's no accident that playwrights from Sophocles and Shakespeare and Molière to Tennessee Williams and Harold Pinter all had some training and background as actors, so they could experience firsthand what the magic of live theatre was all about, and what extraordinary things could be achieved up there onstage.

As for the stage set, costumes, and lighting for a play—we'll deal with all that in a later chapter, but we can say right here that the playwright shouldn't spend too much of his time worrying about such things. There are artisans of the theatre who know the craft of stage design and lighting and costuming much better than any playwright could or should. Besides, in our theatre these production values tend to be over emphasized—what other theatre in the world could you name where an audience applauds the *set* of a play on opening night? Of course that's ludicrous, and we need to go back to what Aristotle tells us about such things, when he reminds us that set design is a very insignificant part of playwriting:

> The spectacle, though an attraction, is the least artistic of all the parts, and has least to do with the art of playwriting. The tragic effect is quite possible without a public performance and actors; and besides, the getting-up of the spectacle is more a matter for the *costumier* than for the playwright.[1]

The most that any playwright needs to know about basic stage design can be summarized in the following list of different types of stage sets:

1. *Box Set:* This uses the "fourth wall," so an audience seems to be looking into one side of a living room, bedroom, courtroom, or any other interior.

2. *Outdoor Set:* This may use a background scrim to represent the sky, a landscape or seascape, or whatever other locale needs to be suggested.

3. *Bare Stage:* This is where the actors themselves suggest what the locale is supposed to be, through their actions and language.

4. *Double House Set:* This originated in the Roman theatre but occurs in certain modern plays such as *Our Town,* where two houses are indicated in the upstage area of the stage.

5. *Special Set:* This will include any extraordinary setting such as the naval rigging on a convoy ship in *Mister Roberts.*

Because after all what is theatre? Scrims and special effects and fourth walls are all very well, but drama is action, and that is what the playwright must concentrate on from beginning to end. Molière said it best: "All I need for a stage is a platform and a couple of passions."

ADVICE FOR PLAYWRIGHTS

Train yourself in the uniform format of playscripting.

SUGGESTED READING

Michel St. Denis: *Theatre: The Rediscovery of Style,* Theatre Arts.

EXERCISES

1. Take a short scene from a play by Shakespeare and try rewriting it in modern playscript format, adding your own minimal character stage directions.

2. Write a short play—then try dividing it into five acts, then three acts, then two acts, and see what difference it makes to the development of your major actions.

3. Build a small stage and locate the different areas—USR, DSR, CS, USL, DSL. See what difference it makes to your play if you reverse the stage designations for the entrances and exits of your characters.

CHAPTER 11

HISTORY OF PLAYS AND PLAYWRITING

Every writer writes alone, but he also writes in an ongoing historical process that has been taking place long before he ever decided to sit down and try to write.

We took a brief look at that historical process in the foreword of this book, and now we can make a quick survey of the 2500 years of world drama, to see what it might be able to say to the practicing playwright about the great shaping forces of theatre. The chronology of plays at the end of this book also contains a fairly extensive listing of outstanding plays from world drama which are recommended for further reading.

Greek theatre began with a curious coalescence of drama, music, poetry, dance, and religion. Thespis created the first onstage actor, Aeschylus created the second actor, and Sophocles created the third actor and raised the number of the chorus from twelve to fifteen persons. All the actors onstage wore masks or white lead make-up, and footwear that added to their height. These actors were not seen as individual characters but as archetypes of mythic heroes and the embodiments of tragic actions. Even so, Greek actors prided themselves on a total immersion in their roles—Plutarch tells how the actor Polus played the role of Electra using the ashes of his dead son in the funeral urn that was supposed to contain the ashes of Orestes.

All the Greek playwrights competed for prizes: Aeschylus won thirteen first prizes, Sophocles won eighteen, and Euripedes won four. Of the hundreds of plays that these three tragic playwrights wrote in their lifetimes, today we have seven plays of Aeschylus, seven plays of Sophocles, and eighteen of Euripedes. In 404 B.C., with the defeat of Athens in the Peloponnesian War, the ensuing disillusionment brought an end to Greek tragedy with its exalted view of human destiny at odds with the will of the gods.

Since the Roman theatre was not consecrated to any god as the Greek theatre was, the Roman stage catered openly to the immediate taste of the public, sometimes with disastrous results. Roman playwrights like Seneca and Plautus and Terence achieved an interesting level of melodrama and rhetoric in their work, but they did not try for anything as sophisticated as the imitation of an action in their plays—often they executed real actions right onstage with shocking cruelty and barbarism. Fellini's film *Satyricon* shows the performance of a Roman play that called for a character to have his hand cut off onstage—and instead of an actor's merely *miming* this stage action, a real prisoner was led out onstage and actually *had* his hand cut off in full view of the audience. Similarly, in the last act of Seneca's *Phaedra*, when the mutilated body of Hippolytus is supposed to be brought onstage, a real wheelbarrow containing actual arms and legs and other body parts is rolled in and Theseus begins reassembling the corpse of his son as if it were a jigsaw puzzle! The low point of Roman theatre probably occurred in 41 A.D., when the robber Laureolus was nailed to a cross onstage in the middle of a mime play. This is not so surprising when we realize that the Romans substituted spectacle for catharsis, and of course the logical consequence of all this was the Colosseum with its gladiatorial contests, wild animal hunts, and tossing Christians to starving lions.

It's no wonder that after the awful excesses of the Roman theatre, the Middle Ages banned theatrical performances altogether, and when the late medieval miracle, mystery, and morality plays were allowed to be staged on pageant wagons, they were carefully restricted to the illustration of church doctrine. Even so, many of these plays show remarkable stagecraft, such as *Everyman* and the 1425 version of *The Second Shepherds Play*.

The English Renaissance lasted for about 40 years as Elizabethan audiences witnessed the first truly poetic dramas since the Greeks. The spirit of humanist learning and openness to new forms, together with the 1455 Gutenberg printing press, made all branches of learning available to everyone, and Shakespeare himself was not above borrowing every plot he ever wrote except for *The Merry Wives of Windsor*. He "lifted" over 3000 lines from other plays to write the second and third parts of *Henry VI*, and he borrowed themes and ideas from Kyd, Lyly, Greene, and Christopher Marlowe. Ben Jonson objected that Shakespeare broke every classical rule including the classical unities of time and place and action; the French later complained that Shakespeare was a tasteless butcher, haphazardly mixing gore and hyperbole and ludicrously juxtaposing comic and tragic styles, such as the macabre murder of King Duncan in *Macbeth*, which is immediately followed by the obscenely funny drunken porter scene. In fact, it was not until a century later that some German critics pointed out the full scope of Shakespeare's genius, and since then he has been the most written-about author in the history of the world. As James Joyce put it in *Ulysses*, "Shakespeare is the happy hunting ground for all minds that have lost their balance."

And it is true that there is hardly any dramatic action or psychic state that Shakespeare did not translate onstage, just as he created onstage visuals that are almost hallucinatory in their power—as when Macbeth sees an imaginary dagger, or Lady Macbeth sees imaginary blood on her hands.

There is no way of gauging the role that the Globe Theatre company played in the creation of Shakespeare's great plays. It is such a rare thing, historically, for a playwright to be both resident author and part-owner of his own ensemble acting company, that we can only speculate on how much the interaction of playwright and actor may have affected the ongoing process of Shakespeare's own playwriting. We'd probably say the effect must have been consider- able, and certainly more than is commonly thought in most academ- ic circles. For example, if we assume that the leading Globe actor, Richard Burbage, played all the diverse and versatile roles that Shakespeare created for him—characters as dissimilar as Romeo, Henry V, Shylock, Brutus, Richard III, Hamlet, Othello, Macbeth, King Lear, and Prospero—we could only dimly imagine how much

Burbage's work in one role may have inspired Shakespeare to go on and create another role so radically different that, in common language, Burbage would have to "sweat for it." "Well, we saw what old Burbage did with Shylock in his Venetian gabardine, and we saw what he did with Brutus in his Roman toga, and we saw what he did with Hamlet in his inky mourning clothes—now let's put the old boy in blackface and see what he does with Othello!" That's the kind of prickly stimulus that sometimes lies behind the greatest enterprises, although of course this is all mere speculation, because the truth is that we know very little of what actually went on in that Globe theatre company.

Meanwhile the Spanish Renaissance had produced playwrights like Lope de Vega and Calderón de la Barca, who was an ordained priest who wrote plays of secular pessimism like *La Vida Es Sueña (Life is a Dream)* where the hero Sagismundo voices the humanist world view of that era:

que toda la vida es sueño,
y los sueños sueños son

for all life is a dream,
and the dreams themselves are dreams

And about the same time, the French neoclassic theatre produced Corneille and Racine with their pure and remorseless re-creations of Greek tragedy, and also the great satirical playwrights Marivaux and Molière, whose plays gave rise to the Comédie-Française, or as it is sometimes affectionately called, "the House of Molière." Molière wrote brave scathing satires such as *Le Misanthrope* and *Tartuffe* and *Le Medicin Malgre Lui,* and he himself died onstage during a performance of *Le Malade Imaginaire,* and the chair he died in is still preserved at the Comédie-Française and is taken on tour whenever the company performs abroad.

Back in England, after Elizabeth's death in 1603, the Jacobean theatre of John Webster became so notoriously agnostic and nihilistic that in 1642 the Puritans finally closed the London theatres and ordered the arrest of all actors as outlaws and vagabonds. And when the Restoration opened the theatres again in 1660, the aristocrats returned from France where they had been admiring the French theatre, and the new Restoration theatre was so heavily influenced by French practices that it was light-years away from the plays of

Shakespeare. Playwrights like Dryden, Congreve, Wycherly, Goldsmith, and Sheridan wrote a middle class prose drama with actresses playing onstage for the first time, and the result was a more domestic comedy of manners and morals, heavy on premises but not so strong on dramatic action or onstage visuals.

The modern theatre of the nineteenth century reflected the tremendous social and political upheavals of the modern world—the American and French revolutions, the enormous technological advances of the Industrial Revolution together with its ruthless exploitation of women and children in sweatshop factories, the adversarial relationship between capital and labor, and the soul-stifling pressures of the new urban civilization. The modern spirit suddenly felt threatened by the loss of almost all its traditional assurances and assumptions, and Romanticism arose to proclaim the lone individual as the sole arbiter of value in the universe. The plays of Ibsen, Chekhov, Gogol, Gorky, Tolstoy, Shaw, O'Neill, Pirandello, Strindberg, Lorca, and Clifford Odets all dramatized the individual's dilemma in trying to adapt and conform to the bewildering complexity and acceleration of the modern world.

And in our contemporary theatre, the plays of Lillian Hellman, Arthur Miller, Tennessee Williams, Edward Albee, and Sam Shepard continue to show the terrible price that an individual has to pay to survive in the modern world. There is even a very highly stylized drama of the twentieth century which has been loosely called "the theatre of the absurd." The plays of Samuel Beckett, Jean Genet, Eugene Ionesco, and Harold Pinter seem to be oblique parables, farces of sadness, stoic jokes, witless riddles, existential jests. These plays all reflect the impact of Freud, who suggested that the great shaping life forces are hidden away inside ourselves in some abyss that we keep concealed far beyond the reach of reason, and can only be dimly glimpsed through the weird imagery of dreams. Man is suffering from a contagion of sadness, he is dumbstruck by the breakdown of language and logic, and he can only make hollow shouts through the joyless void. As Estragon says in *Waiting For Godot*: "Nothing happens, nobody comes, nobody goes, it's awful."

All of these new approaches to drama in the modern world have also given rise to entirely new theories of theatre and performance. Foremost among these theorists was Constantine Stanislavsky, who revolutionized modern acting techniques with his so-called "Method," which is a reaction against the nineteenth century melodrama, full of external acting and theatricality. Stanislavsky's Method stresses an authentic inner emotional technique on the part of the actor, from which everything else proceeds easily and inevitably.

Another theorist who took an almost opposite approach to acting was Bertolt Brecht, who founded the Berliner Ensemble. Brecht trained his actors in the "Verfremdungseffekt" or alienation effect, where an actor seems to be standing outside his part and commenting on it, ironically and even didactically. This approach is especially effective in Brecht's own plays, such as *Mother Courage* and *The Private Life of the Master Race.*

Perhaps the most revolutionary theorist of the modern theatre was the French actor and critic Antonin Artaud. In his book *The Theatre and its Double,* Artaud developed an extraordinary "theatre of cruelty," where all forms were swept away in favor of a searing, immediate, and almost apocalyptic experience. In Artaud's own words, "We are not free. And the sky can still fall on our heads. And the theatre has been created to teach us that first of all."

Together with these radical new theories of theatre, modern drama also gave rise to new training schools and repertory groups in America. The Provincetown Playhouse helped launch the early plays of Eugene O'Neill. In 1931, the Group Theatre was founded by Lee Strasberg, Cheryl Crawford, Harold Clurman, and Elia Kazan. In 1947, the Actors Studio was founded by Robert Lewis and Elia Kazan and Cheryl Crawford. Other American theatre companies of more recent years include The American Place Theatre, The Neighborhood Playhouse, The Roundabout Theatre, and The New York Public Theatre—to say nothing of the innumerable regional theatres that have sprung up across the United States, which are devoted to both a classical repertory and an experimental production of new contemporary playwrights.

Among the outstanding acting schools there is the H.B. Studio founded by Herbert Berghof and Uta Hagen, and a host of individual acting teachers such as Stella Adler, Sanford Meisner, Gene Frankel, Michael Moriarty, Warren Robertson, and Wynn Handman.

As we said at the outset of this chapter, every writer writes alone, but he also writes in an ongoing historical process that is inextricably linked to this tradition of 2500 years of world theatre. It's important for a playwright to have some sense of this ongoing process, not to channel or stifle or oppress him, or even necessarily to exercise any influence over his own original impulses, but simply to make him more aware of what things are possible onstage—and what other things may be absolutely inevitable.

ADVICE FOR PLAYWRIGHTS

Train yourself to know the various resources and techniques of world theatre.

SUGGESTED READING

Richard Boleslavsky: *Acting: The First Six Lessons,* Theatre Arts.

EXERCISES

1. Choose one period of world theatre, and read three plays associated with this period, then write a short play based on the manner of the period.

2. Write a major character action that might be appropriate for the following periods of world theatre: Greek; Roman; Renaissance; Neoclassic; Restoration; nineteenth century; and theatre of the absurd.

3. Imagine you are a resident author in an ensemble acting company and you have to write a short play for an actor whose work you already know very well. Choose a film actor to write for, if you are unfamiliar with the work of a stage actor.

CHAPTER 12

CONTEMPORARY AND AVANT GARDE PLAYWRIGHTS

Now we can begin to look at how actions and visuals and stakes are used by playwrights who are writing in our own contemporary theatre.

First, though, we had better be clear as to what we mean by the word "contemporary." It is more than just a chronological designation, indicating plays that have been written during our own lifetime, or plays that have been written over the last quarter of the twentieth century. The word "contemporary" means a good deal more than that—it goes right to the heart of a new generation that has shared certain profound experiences and has come to certain extraordinary awarenesses. How can we characterize this new generation?

It is a generation that has been nurtured in drama departments and M.F.A. graduate degree playwriting programs, and has had access to travel grants and fellowship awards, and has developed a hip sense of what makes for exciting films and television and theatre.

109

It is a generation that has been radically influenced by television and the electronic media, by cybernetics and computer technology, so it may occasionally wreak havoc with what we like to think of as strict linear logic or the classical unities of time, places, and action. It is a generation of remarkable speed and range and vitality which is trying to give voice to some of the neglected energy principles that are at work in the universe, such as the elements of chance and randomness.

It is a generation that is heir to some of the most momentous social upheavals in history such as the civil rights movement, the sexual revolution, gay rights, women's rights, third world emerging nations, and the ecological crisis. It is a generation that has been raised in the shadow of the maniacal nuclear arms race, and it knows in its soul that we may all be annihilated in the twinkling of an eye. It is a generation that is trying to reflect the bewilderment of an era, a sense of the overwhelming rapid change in all our lives, and the loss of almost all our traditional assumptions and assurances.

Finally, it is a generation that is trying to create a new theatre for our contemporary world, a theatre that can keep up with the acceleration of issues in our time and find some significant mask or stance that may be meaningful in a world that seems to be rapidly estranging itself from the possibility of all meaning.

When we look back over our own modern theatre, to the truly great American playwrights like Eugene O'Neill, and the postwar playwrights like Tennessee Williams and Arthur Miller and Edward Albee, there may be an impatient voice inside us that asks, who of all these new contemporary playwrights will be likely to last? Well, that's always a difficult thing to say, especially today when we're not really sure that any of us will last, because we're not even sure that human civilization will outlast the present century.

In order to learn about the major dramatic forces that have shaped this contemporary American theatre, we need to look at some of the postwar European playwrights who served as forerunners. Following is a list of the European playwrights who probably had the most profound effect on contemporary American playwrights, together with the titles of their most noteworthy plays:

SAMUEL BECKETT: *Waiting for Godot, Happy Days, Endgame, Krapp's Last Tape*

ALBERT CAMUS:	*Caligula*
FRIEDRICH DUERRENMATT:	*The Visit, The Physicists*
JEAN GENET:	*The Blacks, The Balcony, The Maids*
EUGENE IONESCO:	*The Bald Soprano, The Lesson, Jack, Rhinoceros*
HAROLD PINTER:	*The Caretaker, The Homecoming, No Man's Land*

These playwrights are sometimes collectively grouped into the so-called "Theatre of the Absurd," because they write plays that supposedly illustrate and analyze the irrationality of the world around us. And the grouping has some justification, as postwar Europeans have been especially susceptible to the notion of absurdity—this ghastly past half century has exposed them to two wars that were unprecedented in scope and savagery and senselessness. The stalemate trench warfare of World War I, the Warsaw ghetto, Dachau, Belsen, Buchenwald and Auschwitz during World War II—these were all monstrous absurdities, nightmare monuments to the meaninglessness of existence.

It's no wonder, then, that postwar European playwrights began to give voice to their sense of absurdity and abandonment. Albert Camus, writing in *The Myth of Sisyphus,* said man was experiencing "the unspeakable penalty in which the whole being is exerted towards accomplishing nothing." And Eugene Ionesco wrote, "Cut off from his religious, metaphysical, and transcendental roots, man is lost; all his actions become senseless, absurd, and useless."

And when we look at the dramatic work of Beckett, Ionesco, Pinter, and Genet, we can understand how these playwrights all share in the same forlorn premise: That man is suffering from a contagion of sadness, that he is dumbstruck by the breakdown of language and logic, and that he can only make hollow shouts out of a joyless void. So it is no wonder that these absurdist plays are almost all highly stylized, abstract, and melancholy—often no more than elaborate jests, stoic jokes, witless riddles, or plain shaggy dog stories. But beneath their surface absurdity, we sense that these plays are all appalling commentaries on the unspeakable terror of our time.

Without any doubt the most significant, controversial, and enigmatic play of this entire period is Samuel Beckett's *Waiting for Godot,* which was first produced in 1953 as *En Attendant Godot* at the Théâtre de Babylone, directed by Roger Blin. This one play has baffled and fascinated the modern imagination—critics have puzzled over the stark metaphor of "waiting," and audiences have more or less concluded that the play is some sort of oblique parable of man's isolation and abandonment.

The play concerns two tramps, Vladimir and Estragon, who sit and talk endlessly about how futile it is to sit and talk endlessly about how futile it is to sit and talk endlessly. If that sounds circular, it's exactly the case. But Vladimir and Estragon both know that they are also doing something else, something of redemptive importance: they are waiting for Godot. So they wait and wait and wait, and their waiting is punctuated by madcap vaudeville routines, memory lapses, and comic thoughts on suicide and salvation. But always their conversation comes back to the absolute boredom and futility of this existence. As Estragon says, "Nothing happens, nobody comes, nobody goes, it's awful."

They wait and they wait and they wait, and after awhile two new characters, Pozzo and Lucky, enter. Pozzo is taking Lucky to the fair, to sell him (that will be kinder than killing him, he explains). After a long silence, Lucky delivers a nonstop speech of incomparable absurdity, then he falls silent again. Pozzo and Lucky exit, and the tramps continue to wait.

The dialogue of the play is skillful and enthralling, as in this brisk gambit:

VLADIMIR:	What is terrible is to *have* thought.
ESTRAGON:	But did that ever happen to us?
VLADIMIR:	Where are all these corpses from?
ESTRAGON:	These skeletons.
VLADIMIR:	Tell me that.
ESTRAGON:	True.
VLADIMIR:	We must have thought a little.
ESTRAGON:	At the very beginning.
VLADIMIR:	A charnel house! A charnel house!
ESTRAGON:	You don't have to look.
VLADIMIR:	You can't help looking.
ESTRAGON:	True.
VLADIMIR:	Try as one may.
ESTRAGON:	I beg your pardon?
VLADIMIR:	Try as one may.
ESTRAGON:	We should turn resolutely towards Nature.

VLADIMIR:	We've tried that.
ESTRAGON:	True.
VLADIMIR:	Oh it's not the worst, I know.
ESTRAGON:	What?
VLADIMIR:	To have thought.
ESTRAGON:	Obviously.
VLADIMIR:	But we could have done without it.
ESTRAGON:	Que voulez-vous?
VLADIMIR:	I beg your pardon?
ESTRAGON:	Que voulez-vous.
VLADIMIR:	Ah! que voulez-vous. Exactly.

(*Silence*)

| ESTRAGON: | That wasn't such a bad little canter.[1] |

At other times the writing in the play rises to heights of extraordinary eloquence, as in this brief speech:

| VLADIMIR: | . . . Astride of a grave and a difficult birth. Down in the hole, lingeringly, the gravedigger puts on the forceps. We have time to grow old. The air is full of our cries. *(He listens.)* But habit is a great deadener. *(He looks again at ESTRAGON.)* At me too someone is looking, of me too someone is saying, He is sleeping, he knows nothing, let him sleep on. *(Pause.)* I can't go on! *(Pause.)* What have I said?[2] |

What can we make of this heroic nonsense? Beckett himself commented that if he had known who Godot was, he would have said so in the play. Perhaps the most we can say is that the play is a meditation on man's abandonment, and that in waiting for Godot, Vladimir and Estragon are voicing our own mute appeal for pity in a world that is rapidly going to ruin.

The plays of Eugene Ionesco—*The Bald Soprano, The Lesson, Jack or The Submission, Rhinoceros*—are variously described by the playwright himself as "anti-play," "a comic drama," "a naturalistic comedy," and "a tragic farce." The plays are in deadly earnest, yet they have a *buffo* tone, a geometrical cadence, as if they were all luminous and mule-eared farces of sadness.

One play, *Jack or The Submission,* concerns the plight of a young man whose parents insist that he perpetuate all the sacred family patterns by admitting that he loves hashed brown potatoes. It is an absurd demand, and Jack rebels. He will not even tolerate the hypocrisy of language—"Oh words, what crimes are committed in your name!" But his protest can only incur the wrath of his family, and his father erupts in a torrent of ludicrous abuse:

FATHER JACK: You are no son of mine. I disown you. You're not worthy of my ancestors. You resemble your mother and the idiots and imbeciles in her family. This doesn't matter to her for she's only a woman, and what a woman! In short, I needn't elegize her here. I have only this to say to you: impeccably brought up, like an aristocrat, in a family of veritable leeches, of authentic torpedoes, with all the regard due to your rank, to your sex, to the talent that you possess, to the hot blood that can express—if you only wanted it to, all this that your blood itself could but suggest with imperfect words—you, in spite of all this, you show yourself unworthy, at one and the same time of your ancestors, of my ancestors, who disown you for the same reason that I do, and of your descendants who certainly will never see the light of day for they'll prefer to let themselves be killed before they ever come into being. Murderer! Patricide! You have nothing more to envy me for. When I think that I had the unfortunate idea of wishing for a son and not a red poppy![3]

Jack's family pushes Jack into marriage with a surrealistic bride, Roberta, who has two noses on her face and nine fingers on her left hand. Jack pleads with Roberta for understanding, and Roberta sympathizes, but only so she can seduce him. She woos Jack in an illogical language which consists of one word: "cat." At the end of the play, when the lovers finally embrace, Jack's family crawls and waddles back onstage, leering at the young couple and making obscene noises. Ionesco leaves no doubt in our minds about the effect he wishes to create at the end of the play—in his stage directions he writes: "All this must produce in the audience a feeling of embarrassment, awkwardness and shame." In other words, the play is not only a scathing satire of middle class morality, it is also a way of making the audience experience the full impact of absurdity in their own lives.

Ionesco's full-length play *Rhinoceros* was first produced in Paris in 1960 with Jean-Louis Barrault, and it was produced in London in 1960 by Orson Welles with Laurence Olivier playing the part of

Berenger. The premise of the play is that the whole world is going mad and everyone is changing into rhinoceroses:

BERENGER:	All the firemen, a whole regiment of rhinoceroses, led by drums.
DAISY:	They're pouring up the streets!
BERENGER:	It's gone too far, much too far!
DAISY:	More rhinoceroses are streaming out of the courtyard.
BERENGER:	And out of the houses . . .
DUDARD:	And the windows as well!
DAISY:	They're joining up with the others . . .[4]

At the end of the play, Berenger himself feels the strong pull of the herd instinct to transform into a rhinoceros, and his inner struggle is dramatically presented in the following curtain speech:

BERENGER: . . . They're the good-looking ones. I was wrong! Oh, how I wish I was like them! I haven't got any horns, more's the pity! A smooth brow looks so ugly. I need one or two horns to give my sagging face a lift. Perhaps one will grow and I needn't be ashamed any more—then I could go and join them. But it will never grow! *(He looks at the palms of his hands.)* My hands are so limp—oh, why won't they get rough! *(He takes his coat off, undoes his shirt to look at his chest in the mirror.)* My skin is so slack. I can't stand this white, hairy body. Oh I'd love to have a hard skin in that wonderful dull green colour—a skin that looks decent naked without any hair on it, like theirs! *(He listens to the trumpetings.)* This song is charming—a bit raucous perhaps, but it does have charm! I wish I could do it! *(He tries to imitate them.)* Ahh, Ahh, Brr! No, that's not it. Try again, louder! Ahh, Ahh, Brr! No, that's not it, it's too feeble, it's got no drive behind it. I'm not trumpeting at all; I'm just howling. Ahh, Ahh, Brr. There's a big difference between howling and trumpeting. I've only myself to blame; I should have gone with them while there was still time. Now it's too late! Now I'm a monster, just a monster. Now I'll never become a rhinoceros, never, never! I've gone past changing . . . I want to, I really do, but I can't, I just can't. I can't stand the sight of me. I'm too ashamed! *(He turns his back on the mirror.)* I'm so ugly! People who try to hang on to their individuality always come to a bad end! *(He suddenly snaps out of it.)* Oh well, too bad! I'll take on the whole of them! I'll put up a fight against the lot of them, the whole lot of them! I'm the last man left, and I'm staying that way until the end. I'm not capitulating![5]

Jean Genet is a poet of roles and poses, and he delights in stripping masks away to show us our own psychological nakedness. His plays are written for a ritualistic theatre of serious ceremony, halfway between high mass and black magic.

The Balcony begins with a bishop onstage, complete with miter and gilded cope—only this bishop is not really a bishop at all, he is a gasman who has come to Madame Irma's brothel so he can dress up in a bishop's clothes to act out his sexual fantasy of confession, absolution, and atonement. Other customers come to dress up as a judge, who makes a brothel girl stand trial for theft, and a general, who orders a brothel girl to whinny and trot around the room as if she were his favorite horse:

GENERAL: . . . My proud steed! My handsome mare, we've had many a spirited gallop together!

THE GIRL: And that's not all! I want to trip through the world with my nervous legs and well-shod hooves. Take off your pants and shoes so I can dress you.

GENERAL: All right, but first, down on your knees! Come on, come on, bend your knees, bend them . . .

(THE GIRL rears, utters a whinny of pleasure and kneels like a circus horse before the GENERAL.)

GENERAL: Bravo! Bravo, Dove! You haven't forgotten a thing. And now, you're going to help me and answer my questions. It's fitting and proper for a nice filly to help her master unbutton himself and take off his gloves, and to be at his beck and call. Now start by untying my laces.

(During the entire scene that follows, THE GIRL helps the GENERAL remove his clothes and then dress up as a general. When he is completely dressed, he will be seen to have taken on gigantic proportions, by means of trick effects: invisible foot-gear, broadened shoulders, excessive make-up.)[6]

Throughout the play, there is machine gun fire offstage—a revolution is going on, and for political reasons the brothel customers must maintain their fantasy roles and appear on the Balcony as the Bishop, the General and the Judge, in full view of their fellow citizens. Thus these characters have become what they once were only in their mad imaginings—and the audience is baffled at the transformation. Is the Bishop really a bishop after all? The Envoy says it best in the play:

ENVOY: . . . We've reached the point at which we can no longer be actuated by human feelings. Our function will be to support, establish and justify metaphors.

And Madame Irma says to the audience at the end of the play: "You must now go home, where everything—you can be quite sure—will be even falser than here . . ."

The plays of Harold Pinter are ominous, elliptical, and painstakingly understated. One senses there is something of overwhelming importance that is taking place in the subtext, although one can never be quite sure what it is or why we should be so affected by it.

In *The Caretaker*, Aston has invited Davies, a tramp, into his house and offered him a job as caretaker of the premises. Davies is dirty, vicious, and lost, and when Aston reveals to him that he once received electric shock treatments in a mental hospital, Davies seizes on this opportunity to advance himself at Aston's expense. He begins to complain and demand more things—a clock, some new shoes, a bed that is not next to the window. But eventually the stench and the pestering become intolerable, and Davies has to be asked to leave. As the tramp stands there onstage making his pitiful final appeal, suddenly this figure of confusion and connivance becomes inexplicably haunting:

DAVIES: You mean you're throwing me out? You can't do that. Listen man, listen man, I don't mind, I'll stay, I don't mind. I'll tell you what, if you don't want to change beds, we'll keep it as it is, I'll stay in the same bed, maybe if I can get a stronger piece of sacking, like, to go over the window, keep out the draught, that'll do it, what do you say, we'll keep it as it is?[7]

There is no reply, so Davies stands there speechless as the curtain falls, and the audience is dumbfounded, perhaps because it realizes that this filthy tramp is utterly alone and absolutely unable to adapt to any form of human communication or relationship—and that may well be a metaphor for our own contagion of sadness, an echo of our own hollow shouts out of a joyless void.

The work of Albert Camus is perhaps the most articulate statement of our modern predicament. Like St. Augustine who lived 1500 years before him, Camus brought a North African sensibility and perception to essentially European dilemmas and achieved a profound clarity and biting insight into man's forlorn situation.

In his play *Caligula,* Camus depicts the Roman emperor who has lost his mistress Drusilla, and who then undergoes a curious transformation—he tells the senators that from now on he will reign as absolute tyrant. His mistress Caesonia does not understand, and so Caligula tries to verbalize the awful change that is happening to him:

CALIGULA: No, it's no good; you can't understand. But what matter? Perhaps I'll find a way out. Only, I feel a curious stirring within me, as if undreamed-of things were forcing their way up into the light—and I'm helpless against them. *(He moves closer to her.)* Oh, Caesonia, I knew that men felt anguish, but I didn't know what that word anguish meant. Like everyone else I fancied it was a sickness of the mind—no more. But no, it's my body that's in pain. Pain everywhere, in my chest, in my legs and arms. Even my skin is raw, my head is buzzing, I feel like vomiting. But worst of all is this queer taste in my mouth. I've only to stir my tongue, and the world goes black, and everyone looks . . . horrible. How hard, how cruel it is, this process of becoming a man![8]

This blight of the soul is similar to Søren Kierkegaard's idea of the "sickness unto death" which gave rise to modern existentialism —but in this play of Camus', the sickness is made immediately and dramatically relevant to the felt self, so there is no way for us to avoid or ignore it.

The legacy of these postwar European "absurdist" playwrights is evident in the work of our new contemporary American playwrights. Of course there is a whole host of other influences—everything from the dopey pop culture of our television soap operas and comic books and Westerns to the authentic bop rhythms of rock and black jazz, from the nonstop spaciness and pain of our underground drug culture to the sudden death of our impersonal and syndicated gangland killings, from the senseless assassinations of our most idealistic national leaders to the mind-numbing awfulness of our grotesque involvement in the Vietnam War. And out of all these events and influences and lifestyle has come a body of dramatic work that tries to dramatize our contemporary experience.

What follows is, to be sure, an arbitrary listing which represents the author's own choice of the most significant and exciting and lasting contemporary American playwrights, with one representative play listed for each:

DAVID BERRY:	G. R. Point
KENNETH BROWN:	The Brig
ED BULLINS:	The Duplex
CHRISTOPHER DURANG:	Sister Mary Ignatius Explains It All for You
TOM EYEN:	The Theatre of the Eye
JACK GELBER:	The Connection
JOHN GUARE:	The House of Blue Leaves
DAVID HARE:	Plenty
BETH HENLEY:	Crimes of the Heart
JAMES LEO HERLIHY:	Bad Bad Jo-Jo
ISRAEL HOROVITZ:	The Indian Wants the Bronx
ARTHUR KOPIT:	Oh Dad, Poor Dad, Mamma's Hung You in the Closet and I'm Feelin' So Sad
HUGH LEONARD:	Da
DAVID MAMET:	American Buffalo
WILLIAM MASTROSIMONE:	The Woolgatherer
MARK MEDOFF:	Children of a Lesser God
LEONARD MELFI:	Birdbath
JOHN FORD NOONAN:	A Coupla White Chicks Sitting Around Talking
MARSHA NORMAN:	'Night, Mother
JOHN PIELMEIR:	Agnes of God
MIGUEL PINERO:	Short Eyes
DAVID RABE:	In the Boom Boom Room
SAM SHEPARD:	True West
MURRAY SHISGAL:	Jimmy Shine
WENDY WASSERSTEIN:	Uncommon Women and Others
LANFORD WILSON:	Talley's Folly

Now we can look at a few examples of outstanding work by some of these playwrights, in no particular order, to see how they make use of the basic dramatic principles of action and visuals and stakes.

We said that the stage was a visual area, and that this was the most powerful resource that a playwright has at his disposal. In the following scene from *Crimes of the Heart* by Beth Henley, one has to imagine all the various onstage visuals that are at work—it is a *tour de force* of visual writing. Babe has decided to hang herself just as her mother had done, so she leaves the stage and goes upstairs and the kitchen is empty. There is a silence; then a loud, horrible thud is heard from upstairs. The telephone begins ringing onstage, and it continues to ring five times before Babe comes hurrying down the offstage stairs and enters with a broken piece of rope hanging around her neck. The phone continues to ring:

BABE: *(to the phone)* Will you shut up! *(She is jerking the rope from around her neck. She grabs a knife to cut it off.)* Cheap! Miserable! I hate you! I hate you! *(She throws the rope violently around the room. The phone stops ringing.)* Thank God. *(She looks at the stove, goes over to it, and turns the gas on. The sound of gas escaping is heard. BABE sniffs at it.)* Come on. Come on . . . Hurry up . . . I beg you—hurry up! *(Finally, BABE feels the oven is ready; she takes a deep breath and opens the oven door to stick her head into it. She spots the rack and furiously jerks it out. Taking another breath, she sticks her head into the oven. She stands for several moments tapping her fingers furiously on top of the stove. She speaks from inside the oven . . .)* Oh, please. Please. *(After a few moments, she reaches for the box of matches with her head still in the oven. She tries to strike a match. It doesn't catch.)* Oh, Mama, please! *(She throws the match away and is getting a second one.)* Mama . . . Mama . . . So that's why you done it! *(In her excitement she starts to get up, bangs her head and falls back in the stove. MEG enters from the back door, carrying a birthday cake in a pink box.)*

MEG: Babe! *(MEG throws the box down and runs to pull BABE's head out of the oven.)* Oh, my God! What are you doing? What the hell are you doing?

BABE: *(dizzily)* Nothing. I don't know. Nothing. *(MEG turns off the gas and moves BABE to a chair near the open door.)*[9]

The staging of this play will be overwhelmingly powerful because of all the onstage visuals—there is the sound of the offstage thud, then the rope, the knife, the telephone, the stove, the sound of the escaping gas, the matches, and the birthday cake in the pink box. It is a veritable panorama of visuals proclaiming actions of suicide, rescue, catastrophe, and the irony of birthdays.

Another play that has strong onstage visuals is Arthur Kopit's *Oh Dad, Poor Dad, Mamma's Hung You in the Closet and I'm Feelin' So Sad*. A highly stylized, expressionist farce about a killer mother who is intent on emasculating her son, the play satirizes the rites of a perverse matriarchy. In the play, Madame Rosepettle is dictating her memoirs, and she takes walks on the beach where she kicks sand in the faces of young lovers. Her son Jonathan is kept pure and impotent and he finally kills the one girl who might have been a viable mate for him.

All this mayhem is expressed visually in the opening scene, when two bellhops enter a lavish hotel suite carrying a coffin which they put in the master bedroom—the mother has had her husband's corpse stuffed and she carries it around with her as a favorite trophy. She also carries in her entourage a pet piranha and a collection of Venus fly-traps. These bizarre visuals will function as strong symbolic emblems of the cannabilistic libido that is so fiercely at loose in the play.

After visuals, the second basic principle of dramatic writing is strong character action—someone wants something, a clear objective that someone is going for. Sometimes these strong character actions will derive from a major premise which will be an imposed situation that may be set up at the beginning of a play, and then all the powerful conflicts of character actions will proceed from this one major premise.

An example of a play with an unusual major premise that gives rise to strong character actions is *Hopscotch* by Israel Horovitz. The play is set in a playground in Wakefield, Massachusetts, and when the curtain rises we see a young woman playing hopscotch. She jumps from square to square to square, as if she were the only person in the world. But in the distance there is a man watching her. For awhile it looks as if these two people are strangers, but the more they talk, the more it becomes clear that when Elsa was sixteen, Will made her pregnant and then he abandoned her. As the play proceeds, and as we understand more of the premise of the situation, we can sense Elsa's intense hatred for Will behind their seemingly casual banter:

ELSA:	You work anywhere?
WILL:	Yuh. I work.
ELSA:	What kind?
WILL:	I work for a big company . . . Construction.
ELSA:	Oh, really? You construct things?
WILL:	Me, personally? Nope. Opposite. I tear things down. I'm in the destruction end . . . Wrecking.
ELSA:	(*She moves to WILL at bench.*) Gee, it, well, sounds like you've done really well with yourself . . . very successful. (*pauses*) Wrecking, huh? (*pauses*) They pay you a lot of money to do that? (*She sits beside WILL on bench.*)
WILL:	Money? Sure, well . . .
ELSA:	Sounds like it took a lot of schooling . . .
WILL:	Schooling? Well, I . . .
ELSA:	You have a big desk?
WILL:	C'mon . . .

ELSA: . . . a big *position!*
WILL: You s'posed to be *cute* now or somethin'?
ELSA: Me? Cute? Uh-uh. . . .[10]

Another example of strong character action that derives from a major premise is Mark Medoff's play *The Wager*. In the very opening scene of the play, Leeds makes an outrageous proposal to Ward:

LEEDS: *(placing gun and holster in its hiding place on bookshelf)* The wager is double or nothing on the five hundred. The structure of the competition is this: We are *both* betting that you can seduce Honor Stevens. However, if within forty-eight hours after you've first been to bed with her, her husband makes an attempt on your life or kills you, you lose. If he makes an attempt on your life or kills you *after* forty-eight hours, you win. Are you game?[11]

What playwright couldn't get strong character actions out of such a bizarre major premise? The ensuing conflicts and complications will almost proceed of their own accord, with consequences that will be ludicrous or grotesque or tragic, depending on the predilection of the playwright.

The third basic principle of dramatic writing is the use of significant stakes, how much a character cares about what he wants. We can see an excellent example of the introduction of strong stakes in the following scene from David Mamet's play *American Buffalo*. Teach is in Don's Resale Shop and he is planning a robbery with Don for that very evening. So far, so good. Suddenly, in the following brief scene, Teach begins to load a revolver. Now the stakes of the entire play are radically altered, and Don knows it:

TEACH: What time is it?
DON: It's midnight.

           (Pause)

TEACH: I'm going out there now. I'll need the address. *(TEACH takes out revolver and begins to load it.)*
DON: What's that?
TEACH: What?
DON: That.
TEACH: This "gun"?
DON: Yes.

TEACH:	What does it look like?
DON:	A gun.
TEACH:	It *is* a gun.
DON:	*(rises and crosses to center)* I don't like it.
TEACH:	Don't look at it.
DON:	I'm serious.
TEACH:	So am I.[12]

Mamet skillfully shifts the stakes of a dramatic situation in another play, *Sexual Perversity in Chicago*—although this time the shift is almost the opposite of what took place in *American Buffalo,* in which the stakes of a dramatic action were suddenly heightened by the introduction of a loaded revolver. *Sexual Perversity in Chicago* is a study of what happens in contemporary relationships when the stakes are gradually lowered so far that they can only evoke tedium and irritation, as in this scene between a young couple living together:

DANNY:	Do we have any shampoo?
DEBORAH:	I don't know.
DANNY:	You wash your hair at least twice a day. Shampoo is a staple item of your existence. Of course you know.
DEBORAH:	All right. I *do.* Know.
DANNY:	Do we have any shampoo?
DEBORAH:	I don't know. Is your hair dirty?
DANNY:	Does my hair look dirty?
DEBORAH:	Does it feel dirty? *(Pause.)* It looks dirty.
DANNY:	It feels greasy. I hate it when my hair feels greasy.[13]

Sometimes the discovery of something will radically affect the stakes of a play, simply because the characters will know something that they did not know before. In *A Coupla White Chicks Sitting Around Talking* by John Ford Noonan, Hannah Mae is trying to find out whether Maude, her next-door neighbor, made love to Hannah Mae's husband the day before:

HANNAH MAE:	So?
MAUDE:	So?
HANNAH MAE:	Yes or no?
MAUDE:	Yes or no what?
HANNAH MAE:	I need to hear it from you. Did it happen?
MAUDE:	Yes.
HANNAH MAE:	*(taking MAUDE's face in her hands)* Right into my eyes.

MAUDE: Yes, we did it! Yes, yes, yes!! . . .[14]

But sometimes this discovery action will not take place so easily, so the stakes of a play will change more gradually. In John Pielmeier's play *Agnes of God,* a psychiatrist comes to a convent to interview a young nun, Agnes, who is "an unconscious innocent" —she has never read a book, she has never seen a movie, and when she first entered the convent at the age of seventeen, she underwent a curious experience in which she received the stigmata. In the following brief scene, the psychiatrist, Dr. Martha Livingstone, is interviewing Agnes and there is an extraordinarily effective visual in the scene—the psychiatrist's cigarette which she is smoking as she asks Agnes a few questions about her mother:

DOCTOR: She tells you you're ugly?
AGNES: Yes.
DOCTOR: And that you're stupid.
AGNES: Yes.
DOCTOR: And you're a mistake.
AGNES: She says . . . my whole body . . . is a mistake.
DOCTOR: Why?
AGNES: Because she says . . . If I don't watch out . . . I'll have a baby.
DOCTOR: How does she know that?
AGNES: Her headaches.
DOCTOR: Oh yes.
AGNES: And then . . . she touches me.
DOCTOR: Where?
AGNES: Down there. *(silence)* With her cigarette. *(silence)* Please, Mommy. Don't touch me like that. I'll be good. I won't be your bad baby any more. *(Silence. The DOCTOR puts out her cigarette.)*[15]

Sometimes the dialogue in a play will seem to be casual and conversational, but will actually be covering over some tremendously powerful actions and stakes in the subtext of the play. Mark Medoff's play *When You Comin' Back, Red Ryder?* takes place in a diner in the New Mexico desert—it is 6:05 A.M., and Angel has arrived late for the morning shift. Their impatient talk may seem to be insignificant enough, but it's obvious a great deal is brewing beneath the surface. The one strong onstage visual during this scene is Stephen's brown hair:

ANGEL:	Stephen?
STEPHEN:	How many times I gotta tell ya to don't call me Stephen.
ANGEL:	I don't like callin ya Red. It's stupid—callin somebody with brown hair Red.
STEPHEN:	It's my name, ain't it? I don't like Stephen. I like Red. When I was a kid I had red hair.
ANGEL:	But ya don't now. Now ya got brown hair.
STEPHEN:	*(exasperated)* But *then* I did, and then's when counts.
ANGEL:	Who says *then's* when counts?
STEPHEN:	The person that's doin the *countin!* Namely yours truly! . . .[16]

Sometimes the dialogue will express more through tone or style than it will through direct revelation of dramatic action or background information. In Wendy Wasserstein's play *Uncommon Women and Others*, Rita and Samantha are both seniors at Mt. Holyoke College, and in the following scene they engage in a wildly comic mock-macho banter that says more about their reaction to their staid academic situation than any dozens of pages of character description could ever say:

RITA:	Hey, man, wanna go out and cruise for pussy?
SAMANTHA:	Beg your pardon?
RITA:	Come on, man.
SAMANTHA:	*(putting hair brush in her mouth as if it were a pipe)* Can't we talk about soccer? Did you see Dartmouth take us? They had us in the hole.
RITA:	I'd sure like to get into a hole.
SAMANTHA:	Man, be polite.
RITA:	*(gives SAMANTHA a light punch on the arm)* Fuck, man.
SAMANTHA:	*(softly at first)* Shit man. *(She laughs hysterically.)*
RITA:	Fucking "A" man.[17]

Sometimes dialogue will proceed from a cliche situation that is only slightly exagerrated, but the end result will be devastating and hilarious satire of our prevailing social and sexual mores. In the following scene from William Mastrosimone's play *The Woolgatherer*, Cliff is a truck driver who has been invited back to Rose's place. Rose is a salesgirl in South Philadelphia, and her neurasthenic resistance to Cliff's advances makes for an uproariously funny seduction scene:

CLIFF:	Hey, one thing counts out there, Rosie-schmosie. Scratch! And you gotta leap in the fuckin dogfight and grab all you can grab. And while you're out grabbin it, true love's screwin the

	guy next door. And if you lose it, you get true love's consolation prize—alimony payments! So don't hit me with this stale bag of wholesale pigshit about true love because I been there and I know better. *(pause)* Alls I said was I want to hold you and you gotta make a big deal.
ROSE:	It's not my fault I'm this way!
CLIFF:	Look, I don't want to hear about no bad childhood.
ROSE:	I have to be very careful because of my hemophilia.
CLIFF:	Your what?
ROSE:	I happen to have a very very rare blood disease. If I get cut I could bleed to death.
CLIFF:	This ain't happening.
ROSE:	Just a little scratch bleeds for days! And if I get a deep cut, that's it!
CLIFF:	I said I want to hold you, not bite you!
ROSE:	So I have to be very careful![18]

Sometimes dialogue can take the form of an enraptured monologue, in which one character suddenly rises to euphoric heights and encapsulates everything that he wants the other character to know. In John Guare's play *The House of Blue Leaves,* Bunny tells her boyfriend Artie about the vision she has of what could happen during the first visit of a pope to New York City:

BUNNY:	*(ecstatically):* And when he passes by in his limousine, I'll call out, "Your holiness, marry us—the hell with peace to the world—bring peace to us." And he won't hear me because bands will be playing and the whole city yelling, but he'll see me because I been eyed by the best of them, and he'll nod and I'll grab your hand and say, "Marry us, Pope," and he'll wave his holy hand and all the emeralds and rubies on his fingers will send Yes beams. In a way, today's my wedding day. I should have something white at my throat![19]

And finally, dialogue can reflect the fractured ego of a character through the inadvertant dissociation of ideas and the pitiful crippling of syntax, faster than any narrative exposition could ever reveal. In Miguel Pinero's *Short Eyes,* Clark is a middle-class white who has been thrown into the House of Detention for raping a young girl. The Puerto Ricans who share his jail space have nothing but scorn and contempt for him, and Clark realizes his life depends on trying to make himself understood to his fellow inmates—but it all comes out in a mad torrent of broken phrases:

CLARK: Look, what I told you earlier . . . er . . . that between me and you . . . like, I don't know why I even said that, just . . . just that . . . man, like everything was just coming down on me . . . My wife . . . she was at the hospital . . . She . . . she didn't even look at me . . . once, not once . . . Please . . . don't let it out . . . please . . . I'll really go for help this time . . . I promise . . .[20]

Now we've come to several playwrights whose work has achieved considerable stature, importance, and promise for the contemporary American theatre. Foremost of these is Sam Shepard, who is as known to audiences for his individualistic film appearances as he is for his stage plays. But it is in his playwriting that Sam Shepard stands revealed as the most significant major artist of his generation —in his brutal lyric sagas that make for such compelling and berserkly raw drama, alternately comic and tragic tales of our own innate aggression, virtuoso rock gothic allegories of the utter emptiness at the center of the American dream. He has been protean in his output so far, writing terse and inexplicable plays that are as stark as their titles: *Red Cross, Cowboy Mouth, The Tooth of Crime, Buried Child, Fool for Love,* and *Curse of the Starving Class.* Frank Rich says it best about all the plays of Sam Shepard, in his *New York Times* review of the 1985 production of *A Lie of the Mind,* starring Geraldine Page, Amanda Plummer, and Harvey Keitel. Rich writes: "By turns aching and hilarious—and always as lyrical as its accompanying country music—*A Lie of the Mind* is the unmistakable expression of a major writer nearing the height of his powers."

It is in an earlier play, *True West,* that we can see the way Sam Shepard pits the irony of myth against an empty centerless reality. The play is orchestrated to the offstage cries of crickets and coyotes, which punctuate the onstage conflict between two brothers, Lee and Austin. Lee has written the first authentic western in a decade, and now he is trying to con Austin into writing the screenplay version of it. The dialogue is sparse and elliptical, and we are made to feel that there may be more than this one dimension happening onstage:

LEE: You always work by candlelight?
AUSTIN: No—uh—Not always.
LEE: Just sometimes?
AUSTIN: Yeah. Sometimes it's soothing.
LEE: Isn't that what the old guys did?
AUSTIN: What old guys?

LEE:	The forefathers. You know.
AUSTIN:	Forefathers?
LEE:	Isn't that what they did? Candlelight burning into the night? Cabins in the wilderness.
AUSTIN:	I suppose.[21]

Another playwright of considerable achievement and promise for the contemporary American theatre is Christopher Durang, who combines a comic genius for acid satire with a deft sense of what will work theatrically. Durang has written several archetypal plays that explore various spiritual avenues and viewpoints of our modern world, including *The Actor's Nightmare, Beyond Therapy, The Nature and Purpose of the Universe,* and *Titanic*—but he is probably best known for his irreverent and brilliant religious farce, *Sister Mary Ignatius Explains it All for You.*

Sister Mary Ignatius appears onstage in an old-fashioned nun's habit, and she begins to give a lecture to the audience on the catechism of the Roman Catholic Church, especially as it pertains to the cherished doctrines of heaven and purgatory and hell. With the help of her young altar boy assistant, she reads off a list of all those people who will surely be sent to hell, including Brooke Shields, Zsa Zsa Gabor, Mick Jagger, and Roman Polanski. And to justify her mean-spirited parochialism, Sister Mary Ignatius conjures up a vision of the crucified Christ which is so surrealistic and grotesque, it could not possibly have any relevance to the real world except as a weird eternal scarecrow image which serves as some sort of bizarre scapegoat figure:

| SISTER: | . . . Sometimes in the mornings I look at all the children lining up in front of school, and I'm overwhelmed by a sense of sadness and exhaustion thinking of all the pain and suffering and personal unhappiness they're going to face in their lives. *(Looks sad, eats a cookie)* But can their suffering compare with Christ's on the cross? Let us think of Christ on the cross for a moment. Try to feel the nails ripping through His hands and feet. Some experts say that the nails actually went through His wrists, which was better for keeping Him up on the cross, though of course most of the statues have the nails going right through His palms. Imagine those nails being driven through: pound, pound, pound, rip, rip, rip. Think of the crown of thorns eating into His skull, and the sense of infection that He must have felt in His brain and near His eyes. Imagine blood from His brain spurting forth |

through His eyes, imagine His vision squinting forth through
a veil of red liquid. Imagine these things, and then just *dare*
to feel sorry for the children lining up outside of school. We
dare not; His suffering was greater than ours. He died for our
sins! Yours and mine. We put Him up there, you did, all you
people sitting out there. He loved us so much that He came
all the way down to earth just so He could be nailed painfully
to the cross and hang there for three hours. Who else has
loved us as much as that? I come from a large family. My
father was big and ugly, my mother had a nasty disposition
and didn't like me. There were twenty-six of us. It took three
hours just to wash the dishes, but Christ hung on that cross
for three hours and *He* never complained . . .[22]

The play proceeds to a nativity pageant that is put on by Sister
Mary Ignatius and her former students—but the students eventually
turn on the nun and try to embarrass her with what has happened in
their lives since they left the artificial calm and comfort of her
catechism classes. They tell her all about the assorted rapes and
abortions and homosexuality they have experienced in the real
world, and they report their overwhelming sense of abandonment
and randomness in life and nature, which is not taken into account
in any of the traditional teachings of Catholic theology. Sister Mary
Ignatius tries to dismiss all these things, but when the students press
them on her with such force that she cannot ignore them, the nun
shocks the audience by resorting to sudden onstage murder—which
she quickly rationalizes as necessary to retain the structure of a
scholastic Catholic world-view. The play is a reckless spoof and a
blasphemously hilarious romp, but it is much more than this—it is
also a searing indictment of any reactionary church or state teaching
that refuses to take cognizance of all the godawful and harrowing
facts that are all around us always.

Another playwright whose work has placed him in the forefront
of contemporary American theatre is David Rabe. His 1984 play
Hurlyburly was a Broadway hit, and his other plays show his talent for
leaping straight and naked into the blazing hellfire of our modern
world without any preambles or apologies. In his play *The Basic
Training of Pavlo Hummel,* he portrays the brutality and stupidity that
is inflicted by the military on young recruits—the sharp rapid-fire
staccato dialogue, the overlapping and eerie succession of surrealist
scenes, and the mime action of gas masks and hand grenades and
open field discipline. Without flinching, Rabe shows the racism of

the Vietnam War, and what it reveals of the substructure of American society:

CORPORAL: Them slopes; man they're the stupidest bunch a people anybody ever saw. It don't matter what you do to 'em or what you say, man they just look at you. They're some kinda goddamn phenomenon, man. Can of bug spray buy you all the ass you can handle in some places. Insect repellant, man. You ready for that? You give 'em a can a bug spray, you can lay their fourteen-year-old daughter. Not any of 'em screw worth a shit.

And as if that weren't bad enough, Rabe continues to press the point home:

SGT. TOWER: Where you think you are? You think you in the movies? This here real life, Gen'men. You actin like there ain't never been a war in this world. Don't you know what I'm sayin'? You got to want to put this steel into a man. You got to want to cut him, hurt him, make him die. You got to want to feel the skin and muscle come apart with the push you give. It come to you in the wood. RECOVER AND HOLD![23]

In his play *Streamers*, Rabe takes us into the American army barracks during the Vietnam War. Carlyle is a black who likes to bait the trainees, and Richie is a soft-spoken homosexual. In the following scene, Carlyle enters and begins taunting RICHIE:

CARLYLE: You know what I bet. I been lookin' at you real close. It just a way I got about me. And I bet if I was to hang my boy out in front of you, my big old boy, man, you'd start wantin' to touch him. Be beggin' and talkin' sweet to ole Carlyle. Am I right or wrong? *(He leans over RICHIE)* What do you say?
RICHIE: Pardon?
CARLYLE: You heard me. Ohhh, I am so restless, I don't even understand it. My big black boy is what I was talkin' about. My thing, man; my rope, Jim. HEY RICHIE! *(And he lunges, then moves his fingers through RICHIE'S hair)* How long you been a punk? Can you hear me? Am I clear? Do I talk funny? *(He is leaning close)* Can you smell the gin on my mouth?[24]

In another play, *Sticks and Bones*, Rabe depicts an all-American middle class "perfectly happy family" that has all the nice wholesome values of a glossy advertisement. Ozzie and Harriet and Rickie are gathered together at home for the return of David, who has been blinded in the Vietnam War. This family's well-intentioned attempts to get in touch with their blind son and his war experiences are awkward and embarrassing:

> "Their skins are yellow, aren't they?"
> "They eat the flesh of dogs."[25]

And in another play, *In the Boom Boom Room,* Rabe explores the character of Chrissy, who is a go-go dancer with aspirations to be a great dancer. She is attractive, naive, and longs for pop romance that will take her away from a humdrum life. In a way, Chrissy represents everything that is wrong with the American dream—because behind all the cha-cha rhythms of a go-go dancer, Chrissy knows there is a profound hatred of life itself. In the following scene, Chrissy goes to work on her mother Helen, for what took place during Helen's pregnancy:

CHRISSY: . . . I hear your thinkin' how I am hateful, all these rays a hate sent in at me into my head! *(And she falls to her knees)* SHUT UP, SHUT UP! You ain't tellin' me anymore. You are done tellin' me. You tried to get rid of me, and you ain't changin' it now. You used to sit on the floor and bounce up and down tryin' to get me out like a hunk a ole blood in that belly and so that's how you always looked at me and me at myself, like I was a little bit dead or that oughta be dead, which is how I regard and look at myself a lot. But I don't oughta be dead. I mean, Christ almighty, sometimes I think about what it musta been to be me inside you bouncin' up and down and I wasn't ready to come out. I would only die if I did. How did I feel? How did I feel? *(She has bounced on the floor; she has fallen forward.)*[26]

Perhaps the most devastating play about America's involvement in the Vietnam War and what it did to an entire generation of Americans, is David Berry's play *G. R. Point.* "G. R." stands for the Graves Registration area, where corpses are brought for final processing before burial. In the following scene, Micah Bradstreet has just experienced his first battle, during a Viet Cong attack, and he is still staggering under the shock of realization that he has personally killed a large number of Vietnamese:

MICAH: *(icily in control)* Zan . . . they're all fucken liars . . . smart fucken liars . . . fucking whoring lies right down to me. Fucken imposters! They didn't tell me . . . they . . . *liked* . . . the blood. I LIKED THE BLOOD!! *That's* a man, huh? That's a *man*.

(pause)

Out there, man . . . raggedy gook bodies with stiff blooming cocks seeping semen, Zan . . . bloody rigormorising cocks fucking the obscene air . . .

(pause)

"Dear mother, I want to tell you about corpse cocks." MOTHER!! Don't touch me, Zan! "Dear Mother—"

ZAN: Cut the crap, Micah!

MICAH: They're out there now picking up the bodies *I* made!

ZAN: That's right—

MICAH: This morning, almost dawn, this morning just before the end, I got three of 'em with my fougas, three of 'em, fucken scared kids, I got 'em with my crazy-gas, deep fried 'em with my napalm barrel, they were fucking *hiding* behind the barrel! They almost made it to the end, but I pushed the button AND I MELTED THEM!!! I did that. I burned those gook kids, didn't I?

ZAN: Uh-huh, you did. But we all did, Micah. Everybody pushes the same button.

MICAH: Zan . . . I . . .

ZAN: Yes, Micah?

MICAH: *(rising)* Man, I fucken *begged* Charlie to come for me! Come for me, you motherfuckers, I'm gonna tear your throats! Get near me, you bastards, and I'm gonna eat you, gonna cut open your fucken stomachs 'n wrap your steaming guts around my neck 'n rip your veins wide open and drink your warm blood 'n pound your fucken heads on the bunker beams 'til there's nothing fucken left of you for G. R. to shovel into the truck and take to the dump and push into a hole and pour diesel on and burn, you motherfuckers, BURN!!!

ZAN: Easy, man, easy.

MICAH: I had . . . I had . . . I want to get clean! I stink!

ZAN: You smell alive.

MICAH: Zan! The bunker was hit next to me and I couldn't hear anything anymore and the colors rushed into me and out of me and I slammed home clips and sprayed beaucoup shit and no more fear anymore and no more wanting to piss and I couldn't hear anything anymore except in my head, every-thing was alive and breathing in the dark—I'm so fucken dirty—I've never been alive like that . . . I was alive . . . I have to wash . . . so alive . . . and I . . .

(He suddenly grabs ZAN, then lurches away)

   . . . I had . . . I killed all those people and . . . I had . . . I . . . I . . .

ZAN: *(shaken) What,* Micah? What?

MICAH: I CAME!!! *(pause)* In the middle of that . . . I came. Like some animal . . . *(ZAN begins to hold him. MICAH resists but ZAN doesn't let go.)* . . . filthy . . . DON'T TOUCH ME . . . don't. Please . . . don't . . . please . . . don't . . . touch . . . me . . . please . . .[27]

Finally, one of the most talented and promising of American playwrights, Marsha Norman, received wide critical and artistic acclaim for her powerful exploration of contemporary womanhood, *'Night, Mother.* In an earlier play, *Getting Out,* Norman similarly probes the mind life of a young woman, Arlene, who remembers herself as a young girl. In the words of the playwright, "Arlie is the violent kid Arlene was until her last stretch in prison . . . Arlie, in a sense, is Arlene's memory of herself, called up by fears, needs and even simple word cues."

ARLIE: So, there was this little kid, see, this creepy little fucker next door. Had glasses an somethin wrong with his foot. I don't know, seven, maybe. Anyhow, ever time his daddy went fishin, he'd bring this kid back some frogs. They built this little fence around em in the back yard like they was pets or somethin. An we'd try to go over an see em but he'd start screamin to his mother to come out an git rid of us. Real snotty like. So we got sick of him bein such a goody-goody an one night me an June snuck over there an put all his dumb ol frogs in this sack. You never heard such a fuss. *(Makes croaking sounds.)* Slimy bastards, frogs. We was plannin to let em go all over the place, but when they started jumpin an all, we just figured they was askin for it. So, we taken em out front to the porch an we throwed em, one at a time, into the street. *(Laughs)* Some of em hit cars goin by but most of em jus got squashed, you know, runned over? It was great, seein how far we could throw em, over back of our backs an under our legs an God, it was really fun watchin em fly through the air then SPLAT *(Claps hands)* all over somebody's car window or somethin. Then the next day, we was waitin and this little kid comes out in his back yard lookin for his stupid frogs and he don't see any an he gets so crazy, cryin and everything. So me an June goes over an tells him we seen this big mess out in the street, an he goes out an sees all them frogs legs and bodies an shit all over the everwhere, an, man, it was so funny. We bout killed ourselves laughin. Then his mother come out and she wouldn't let him go out an pick up all the pieces, so he jus had to stand there watchin all the cars go by smush his little babies right into the street. I's gonna run out an git him a frog's head, but June yellin at me "Arlie, git over here fore some car slips on them frog guts an crashes into you." *(Pause)* I never had so much fun in one day in my whole life . . .[28]

All these contemporary American playwrights are trying to evolve a strenuous and outspoken theatre that will be relevant to our present situation. Against the ghastly European experience of the holocaust, these American playwrights pit the utter cynicism and futility of our involvement in the Vietnam War—and they also mix their strong sense of absurdity and meaninglessness with a lively dose of pop/rock culture, television media hype, and a renewed awareness of the role of chance and randomness in the universe. These contemporary American playwrights go on trying to write plays that reflect the bewilderment of our era, if only because our only hope is in a full consciousness of our predicament.

ADVICE FOR PLAYWRIGHTS

Read as many contemporary plays as you can, and try to see as many contemporary plays as possible.

SUGGESTED READING

The plays of any of the playwrights who are mentioned in this chapter.

EXERCISES

1. Choose one of the brief scenes in this chapter and make a list of the major actions, the onstage visuals, and the stakes that are contained within the scene.

2. Choose one of the European playwrights who are discussed in this chapter and try to write a brief scene that is in the same style as this playwright.

3. Do the same with one of the American playwrights who is described in this chapter.

CHAPTER 13

THE PROCESS OF PLAYWRITING

The process of writing varies from one writer to another writer so radically, and the creative temperament is so notoriously obstreperous and refractory, it would be foolish for us to try and give anyone any advice on the actual practice of how to write a play. The most we can do here is to set down certain clear and simple approaches, if only to show the wide variety of ways that different playwrights have gone about their playwriting.

First of all, as to the rate and pace of writing—it will vary tremendously, depending on the personality and the circumstances of the individual writer. We know that during the classical period, Aeschylus wrote a total of 90 plays, Sophocles wrote a total of 125 plays, and Euripedes wrote between 80 and 92 plays. This extraordinary output of creative work by these great Greek playwrights is all the more remarkable when we consider that they all wrote their plays under the most extraordinary circumstances. Aeschylus, for example, fought at the Battle of Marathon in 490 B.C., and he considered this event a much more significant achievement in his life than the writing of any of his plays, even the soaring *Oresteia*. As Aeschylus tells us on his tombstone: "This monument hides Aeschylus, son of Euphoria, an Athenian, who passed away in wheat-bearing Gela. His fighting strength the grove of Marathon might tell, and the Mede with long hair who came to know it." Not one word about any of the plays he wrote, or the first prizes he won! And Sophocles wrote his great *Oedipus at Colonus* at the age of ninety, and he even read portions of this play out loud in a court of law to prove his competence when his seventy year old son accused the aging playwright of senility. And there is no telling how much Euripedes suffered from the taunts and ridicule of Aristophanes, who said he was a boring bookworm and a cynical woman-hater—all we know for sure is that Euripedes only won four first prizes for all his plays, and his great masterpiece *Medea* earned him a mere third prize—he ended his life in self-imposed exile in Macedonia.

During the Renaissance, Shakespeare wrote 36 plays at an average rate of two plays per year, alternating from comedy to history to tragedy, and in the years 1605–1606 he achieved the astonishing feat of writing *Macbeth* and *King Lear* back to back. What can we say of this prodigious work rate of Shakespeare? We know very little of the way Shakespeare actually wrote—Ben Jonson claimed he never saw Shakespeare blot out a single line, but there is always the strong possibility that Shakespeare had no intention of letting Ben Jonson know anything about his work habits. All that we really have is a telling self-portrait in the final chorus of *Henry V*, where Shakespeare modestly describes himself as a man sitting alone in a small room, leaning over his writing table:

> Thus far, with rough and all-unable pen,
> Our bending author hath pursu'd the story;
> In little room confining mighty men,
> Mangling by starts the full course of their glory . . .[1]

"Our bending author"—that's the only real description we have of William Shakespeare at work, but it makes perfect sense and it gives us some idea of the monumental solitary labor that must have gone into the making of all those great plays. As for the endless hammering out of the form in his work, Ben Jonson says it best in his poem to Shakespeare:

Who casts to write a living line must sweat,
(Such as thine are) and strike the second heat
Upon the Muses' anvil: turn the soul
(And himself with it) that he thinks to frame;
Or for the laurel he may gain a scorn,
For a good poet's made as well as born.
And such wert thou . . .[2]

The rates of writing of the other Renaissance playwrights are just as difficult for us to assess—Molière wrote 29 plays and Racine wrote only 9 plays, but Lope de Vega was so prolific that he wrote from 1500 to 2000 plays, some of them in twenty-four hours.

And in our modern world, it's impossible to come up with any uniform writing rate—Gorky wrote 20 plays and Pirandello wrote 44 plays, but Ibsen spent two years working on *A Doll's House* and Goethe spent almost sixty years working on his *Faust*.

There can be no rule as to the rate and pace of anyone's playwriting, just as there can never be any accurate appraisal of what goes to make up the peculiar genius of a playwright. It's almost embarrassing that after 2000 years we still know so little about the psychology of the playwright. Plato may have said it all when he claimed the artist had to be slightly deranged:

> But he who, having no touch of the Muse's madness in his soul, comes to the door and thinks he will get admitted into the temple of art—he, I say, and his poetry are not admitted; the sane man disappears and is nowhere when he enters into rivalry with the madman.[3]

Aristotle tempers this a little when he says that playwriting requires either genius or a certain type of madness:

> Given the same natural qualifications, he who feels the emotions to be described will be the most convincing; distress and anger, for instance, are portrayed most truthfully by one who is feeling them at the moment. Hence it is that poetry [i.e., playwriting] demands a man with a special gift for it, or else one with a touch of madness in him; the former can easily assume the required mood, and the latter may be actually beside himself with emotion.[4]

Whichever kind of personality one happens to be, Aristotle gives us an interesting description of the actual process of playwriting itself:

> At the time when he is constructing his plots, and engaged on the diction

in which they are worked out, the poet should remember to put the actual scenes as far as possible before his eyes. In this way, seeing everything with the vividness of an eyewitness as it were, he will devise what is appropriate, and be least likely to overlook incongruities . . . As far as may be, too, the poet should even act his story with the very gestures of his personages . . .[5]

This is about as graphic a description of the act of playwriting as we'll probably ever have—first, the playwright must get himself into some sort of trance state so he really sees what is taking place onstage; and then, the playwright must re-create the actions of all his characters, becoming each one of them in an improvisational miming of the way these characters would move, talk, and behave on that same stage.

It's no easy feat to enter into this kind of an easy freedom where there are no inhibitions to keep from being what one imagines oneself to be. First of all, there are all the conventional restraints of not making a fool of oneself—and those are the first inhibitions that will have to go, if one is to be a really effective playwright. Then there are the much deeper inhibitions that have to be dealt with, the repressions that keep one from revealing all the various areas of awareness that are inside oneself, hidden away far in the darkness of the heart.

Then if one can achieve this extraordinary degree of freedom in one's own imagination, there is still one last inhibition to be dealt with which is perhaps the most difficult of all. And this last inhibition is the fear of madness—that very madness that Plato warned us of, the fear that one may free oneself so completely from all one's conventional restraints and from all one's inhibitions about revealing oneself, that one might not be able to come back to the everyday world of clocks and telephones and dental appointments. And this is indeed a very real problem, for each person to confront on his own terms.

Because what can anyone say about this last threshold of inhibition, this very real fear of madness one encounters when one goes as far as one can go into the process of writing?

Of course it will always depend on how badly one really wants to write, and how much one is willing to risk to be able to write a play that is at all worthwhile. But it might be useful to look at the question from another point of view: that of experience, which tells us that there is much more likelihood of someone's going mad if one does *not* continually explore all these concealed realities inside the self, than if one does explore them.

It's also an interesting irony that the very cornerstone of our modern psychoanalytic theory is derived from ideas relating to the Oedipus complex and the Electra complex—both creations of playwrights who were able to portray the stark drama of the human psyche in extraordinary visual and dramatic terms. It's as if one has to overcome one's fear of madness, if one is ever to discover any authentic measure of what sanity itself is all about.

And indeed we can see this heroic effort to overcome one's own fears, inhibitions, and restraints in our greatest theatre artists. Stanislavsky reminds us of the pain of creative labor, in trying to create a character:

> The worst of all human tortures are the pangs of creation. They are the true tortures of Tantalus. You feel the something that is lacking in the part; it is very near, here in yourself, and all you have to do is take hold of it, but as soon as you stretch your hand it is gone.[6]

And Ibsen reports the great pain his plays cost him—"All that I have written over these last ten years, I have lived through spiritually." Ibsen also thrived on the bitter rivalry he felt with the Swedish playwright Strindberg, whose picture he kept over his desk. Ibsen once commented, "He is my mortal enemy and shall hang there and watch me as I write."

Tennessee Williams reports in his *Memoirs* how he was enrolled at the University of Iowa when he learned with horror that his parents had authorized a lobotomy operation on his sister Rose at a Missouri state asylum; Williams subsequently left college in 1938, severed his family ties, and devoted himself to a lifetime of writing.

One might say these are radical examples of crisis and shock and rivalry, and not always typical of the process of writing. Even so, the Spanish playwright Garcia Lorca advocated just such a life of brutal confrontation with reality for any artist who was at all serious in his aims—"For poets and playwrights, I would organize attacks and challenges, instead of tributes."

As for the more technical problems associated with the process of writing, following are six special areas of concern to every practicing playwright:

1. *Beginnings.* It's a cliche to say that the best way for anyone to learn how

to do something is just to plunge in, the same way one tosses a child into the water to "teach" him how to swim—because the most that kind of approach ever results in is a rather uninteresting kind of dogpaddling.

Even so, the truth is the only way to begin to do a thing is to begin to do it. One must have the courage to open a notebook and begin writing and see where the writing wants to take one. And the most important thing is never to let oneself get frozen motionless over any one project, but to keep one's sense of the ongoing process always. As Chekhov put it: "Don't write a play; write plays."

In other words, keep the process going, endlessly and forever. As the poet William Blake said: "Without unceasing Practise nothing can be done. Practise is Art. If you leave off you are lost."

2. *Blocks.* Who hasn't experienced a block? We've all known these stone cold walls of the soul, and we've all sat and stared at a blank page of paper.

The best way out of a block is to begin writing about the block itself—where it came from, what it may be trying to tell you, and how much you wish it would go away. Chances are that this kind of direct confrontation will usually reveal some clue as to the true nature of the block, and give one the key to resolving it. But again, one really has to want to keep on with the process of writing.

William Inge once asked Tennessee Williams if he didn't feel blocked as a writer, and Williams replied: "Yes, I do, I've always been blocked as a writer, but I love writing so much that I always break through the block."

3. *Dry Periods.* Dry periods occur when a block continues over an inordinate period of time, and no amount of notebook exercising can get one out of it. This happens to many writers, and the best thing is to accept it for what it is—a period of non-writing, and not to let oneself get despondent about it.

It really all depends on what one means by "writing." Writing is a far more complex and mysterious process than merely inscribing words on a page, and it can be going on inside of one secretly, deeply, without one's even being aware of it.

Arthur Miller went from writing the screenplay of *The Misfits* through seven years of non-writing until he finally wrote his play *After the Fall*—and when he was asked about this extraordinary dry period, Miller replied: "A writer ought to have the right to shut up when he has nothing he feels he must say; to shut up and still be considered a writer."

4. *Workshop Situations.* Worthwhile playwriting seminars are few and far between, and sometimes mediocre ones can do more harm than good to a young playwright. But if he can locate a tolerable workshop or seminar situation somewhere, a playwright will always benefit from seeing his play mounted and given staged readings so he can get actor and audience feedback.

Many schools and universities have committed themselves to experimental drama programs, and a playwright can benefit from these if he stays clear of the academic and theoretical side of such programs.

He can also travel to all of the great world theatres and theatre schools around the world—in England there is RADA (Royal Academy of Dramatic Arts), LAMDA (London Academy of Music and Dramatic Arts), the Guildhall School, and the Central School; in Berlin there is the Berliner Ensemble and the Max Reinhardt Schule; in Paris there is the École Dullin and the Conservatoire of the Comédie-Française; in Sweden there is the School of Royal Dramatic Theatre; in Russia there is the Moscow Art Theatre Studio School; and in Japan there are the Kabuki and Noh theatre troupes.

But for all of one's traveling and schooling, it's also good for the playwright to keep in mind what Hemingway said in his 1954 Nobel Prize acceptance speech: "Writing at its best is a lonely life. Organizations for writers palliate the writer's loneliness, but I doubt if they truly improve his writing . . . For he does his work alone, and if he is a good enough writer, he must face eternity, or the lack of it, each day."

5. *Autobiographical Writing.* One will always write about oneself, about the things that one knows and loves and believes. But if a play is too literally autobiographical, it will sometimes tend to paralyze the major actions of the play, because one is too close to it.

Aristotle warns of this in the *Poetics* when he says: "The poet (playwright) should say very little *in propria persona* (in his own voice), as he is no imitator when he is doing that." The best way around this problem is for the playwright to distance himself from a character that may be too literally autobiographical, by changing the character's age or race or sex or social status, so the playwright will no longer be so strictly identified with that character.

The problem of narcissism is always a danger in any art form, and the best way of checking it in the theatre is to bear in mind what Stanislavsky once said: "Love the art in yourself, not yourself in the art."

6. *Work Habits.* Writers tend to be idiosyncratic and eccentric in their individual work habits. Racine claimed he composed the whole of *Phèdre* in his head before he set down a single word of it—whereas Tennessee Williams claimed he wrote every morning of his adult life, wherever he was, composing the dialogue out loud as he paced back and forth across the floor, talking to himself so he could hear how the lines sounded.

What matters, of course, is how one goes about getting the best results, and that will vary from writer to writer. All that's important is that each writer know his own work habits, and try to keep to them as faithfully as he can.

As we said at the outset of this chapter, the process of writing varies from writer to writer so radically, it would be foolish for us to set down any rules about the actual practice of writing for everyone.

We can, however, offer the following checklist of basic dramatic principles based on the approach that is outlined in this book. It will probably be useful for a playwright to test any work in progress by going through this checklist with his new play in mind, to see which areas may need further exploration and development:

1. *Opening beat:* Is this the best possible beginning for my play?

2. *Exposition:* Do I have all the necessary background material—prior actions, offstage actions, and given circumstances?

3. *Action:* What is the major through-line action of the entire play?

4. *Characters:* What does each character in my play want?

5. *Obstacles:* What are the obstacles to each character's getting what he wants?

6. *Stakes:* How badly does each character want what he says he wants?

7. *Visuals:* Are the dramatic actions of each character embodied in strong clear visuals?

8. *Dialogue:* Does it advance the major action of the play?

9. *Motifs:* Do they express the underlying dramatic themes of the play?

10. *Climax:* Is there a turning point or a reversal or a major discovery?

11. *Ending.* Is this the best possible ending for my play?

12. *Title.* Is this the best possible title for my play?

ADVICE FOR PLAYWRIGHTS

Train yourself in the ongoing process of writing, at whatever rate or pace you feel is appropriate to your best work.

SUGGESTED READING

Tennessee Williams: *Memoirs,* Doubleday, 1972.

EXERCISES

1. Check out all the playwriting workshop situations in your area, audit them, and then write a summary of the different approaches to the problem of playwriting.

2. Write a list of all the blocks that have ever occurred in your own ongoing process of writing.

3. Use the playwriting checklist at the end of this chapter for one of your own plays, to rewrite any parts of it that may need strengthening.

AFTERWORD

PLAY PRODUCTION

We left this for last: what happens to a play when it goes into production; what happens to the playwright when he comes face to face with the actors who are cast in his play, and the director whose job it is to stage the play; and what happens when the playwright meets with the other professional colleagues who will work on the play production—the scenic designer, the lighting designer, the costume designer, and the producer.

And then what happens when the playwright faces the opening night of his play, and sees and feels its effect on a live audience; and what happens when the playwright reads the reviews of his play written by the drama critics.

Of course, all of this will vary with individual experiences from production to production, so it's not possible for us to lay down any firm rules for what a playwright should or should not do when he is faced with having his play produced in this most collaborative of all the arts.

143

First of all, there is the problem of how a playwright should go about getting a production of his play in the first place. He may have to xerox dozens of copies of his playscript and circulate them among actors and directors and producers and agents and actors and other "contact" persons, until he is able to interest someone in doing his play. And even then, he may have to arrange for a staged reading or a backer's showcase of the play, to get the necessary support to take the play into full production.

Then the question arises as to the playwright's relation to his other working theatre colleagues.

It's true that the playwright has created the original playscript, and that will become the working text for any full production. But that's only the first step. As we said, the playscript is really no more than a sort of musical score which still has to go through endless interpretations by countless persons, before it can be brought to full realization in an onstage production. And along the way, there may be countless changes, cuts, rewrites, interpolations, additions, and alternations of the original text. There will be hardly anyone involved in this collaborative venture who will not want to have his own creative input and suggestions as to how the original playscript can be made "better."

So the question really boils down to this: when should a playwright yield to script changes, and when should he fight to keep his playscript the way he originally wrote it?

It's not an easy question to answer, and in the long run whether a playwright will be open to changes that may or may not be improvements may depend a good deal on the individual temperament of the playwright.

The most we can do here is set down certain descriptions of the different professional areas that are involved in play production, and give some indication as to how a playwright should approach each one of them. These different professional areas are: the actors, the director, the scenic designer, the lighting designer, the costume designer, the producer, the audiences, and the drama critics.

1. THE ACTORS

In ideal circumstances, a playwright should have casting approval, or at least he should be consulted as to the choice of actors who will be performing in his play. In actual practice, whether he is offered this privilege and authority depends on what kind of production contract the playwright has. Many playwrights, because of their lack of experience in the professional theatre, may find themselves facing a production that has already been pre-cast without their knowledge or approval, and when that happens they can either veto the whole thing or else stand aside and hope it all works out for the best.

But assuming that a director has respect for a playwright's opinion and wants to involve him in the process of casting a play, then the playwright will be present during the preliminary auditions and interviews, when actors come to try out for the various roles in the play. And then the playwright may also be a part of the meetings between the director and the producer, and help decide which actors will balance out the cast and give the best interpretation of the play.

Once a play goes into rehearsals, the playwright has a right to expect that the actors will learn his lines word for word, with no paraphrasing or dropped words or switched phrasings. In actual practice, this will depend a good deal on the director's being willing to enforce the memorization of the play text exactly as the playwright originally wrote it.

And if a playwright is allowed to sit in on the actual rehearsals of his play and watch the actors as they begin to take on the life of their characters, a playwright will experience something quite extraordinary. He will suddenly realize that it is no longer "his" play —because the play is on its way to belonging to the actors. And when this happens, sometimes it takes a psyche of steel for a playwright to restrain himself, as the actors go groping for their separate roles. In fact a playwright will probably witness so many improvisational gambits on the part of the actors, he will wish he could get up there onstage himself and tell the actors the way they ought to do it—just as Hamlet the "playwright" unleashed a torrent of instruction on certain "unready" players who were about to perform one of his own speeches onstage:

> Speak the speech, I pray you, as I pronounced it to you, trippingly on the tongue; but if you mouth it, as many of your players do, I had as lief the town-crier spoke my lines. Nor do not saw the air too much with your hand, thus; but use all gently; for in the very torrent, tempest, and (as I may say) whirlwind of passion, you must acquire and beget a temperance, that may give it smoothness. O! it offends me to the

soul to hear a robustious periwig-pated fellow tear a passion to tatters, to very rags, to split the ears of the groundlings; who, for the most part, are capable of nothing but inexplicable dumb shows and noise. I would have such a fellow whipped for o'erdoing Termagant; it out-herods Herod; pray you avoid it . . .[1]

All this fury and anger and instruction may be going on inside a playwright as he sits and watches the actors rehearsing his play, and he may be extremely reluctant to yield his play up to them—but yield he must, if his work is ever to take on the collaborative life that is needed for a full performance in the theatre.

At about this point in rehearsals, people will begin asking the playwright for changes. The actors will complain about certain lines, and the director will insist on certain other changes, and the stage manager may even point out certain inconsistencies of writing from one scene to another. At this point the playwright should be in strong control of his own understanding of the play, so he will know which changes he should make and which changes he should resist making.

From a legal point of view, the playwright is protected from anyone's making any unwarranted changes behind his back. The current Dramatists Guild contract specifies that no changes can be made in any play text without the written permission of the playwright.

That's all very well, but as we said, the rehearsal pressures will still be there, and the playwright will still have to decide what he chooses to change and what he chooses to keep as it is.

It is the duty of the production stage manager to maintain a master playscript copy at all times, with all the changes and cuts and new material that has been added during the rehearsal period. We can say as a matter of record that by the time any play opens, that stage manager's book will always look considerably different from the original playscript text that the playwright started out with. That happens to be the way things are in our theatre, and it will usually always be nerve-wracking and unsettling for a playwright to endure the pressures of the process of production changes that are bound to take place as a play begins to take shape onstage.

But how and when and where the playwright should choose to make changes, or allow others to make changes in his original playscript—that will always have to remain a matter for his own judgment.

2. THE DIRECTOR

It is the plain truth that some directors feel nervous and insecure when playwrights are present during the rehearsal period. And these directors will sometimes do anything they can to get rid of the playwrights, because they sense a deep rivalry as to who really owns the rights to the subtextual interpretation of the play—the director or the playwright.

Part of the reason for this is historical. "Directors" did not become a significant part of our theatre until a couple of centuries ago. Notice in the passage from Hamlet that we quoted above, he says he has just "pronounced" his lines to the actors—in other words, he, the playwright, was serving as the "director" of his own work, giving line readings and instructing the actors on how they should deliver their parts. Directors did not come into the Western theatre until the eighteenth century, and since then the precise function of the director in a play production has never really been very clearly defined. On the one hand there is the theory that a director is no more than an interpreter of the playwright's intention, someone whose job it is to mount the play as nearly as possible to the way the playwright originally conceived it. And on the other hand there is the theory that the director is an "auteur" in his own right, which means the director is the true creator of the final performance of the play, regardless of what the playwright may or may not have written in his original playscript text. Most experiences that playwrights have with directors will fall somewhere between these two radical extremes of the director as interpreter, and the director as "auteur."

Now it is true that directors can work magic with a playscript, but it is equally true that a director can wreak havoc and mayhem with the same playscript. To the extent that a playwright can strike a creative and collaborative relationship with a director, there is at least the possibility of a give and take exchange of ideas and intuitions. And that is always the most rewarding state of affairs, to produce a truly collaborative final performance of the play.

And after all, no matter how grievously a playwright may feel a director is misunderstanding and misinterpreting his playscript, he should always remember that as great a playwright as Chekhov never saw eye to eye with as great a director as Stanislavsky. After the first production of Chekhov's play *The Sea Gull,* Stanislavsky admitted he had never seen "the essence, the aroma, the beauty" of the play

—and when the play was first produced in St. Petersburg in 1896, Chekhov was so shattered by the misunderstanding of his original intentions, that he ran out of the theatre and spent the rest of the night by the Neva River, vowing he would never write plays again or try to have them produced, not even if he lived to be 700 years old!

And in our own theatre, a director as great as Elia Kazan did not always see eye to eye with as great a playwright as Tennessee Williams. Williams admits that Kazan was probably the only director who saw how desperately much Williams' work meant to him. But when *Cat on a Hot Tin Roof* was produced on Broadway, Kazan prevailed on Williams to rewrite the last act of the play completely. And to this day the published text of the play has alternate endings—the one that Williams originally wrote, and the one that Kazan prevailed on Williams to write.

What should we make of all this? Where does the playwright's authority end, and where does the director's authority begin? The question will probably never be answered in our lifetime, and the most we can say here is this: the playwright's authority consists in writing the original playscript, and he should try to exert as much directorial control over the actions and visuals in his play text as he can, so there will be no possibility of misunderstanding or misinterpretation once the play itself goes into rehearsals.

In other words, we are recommending that the playwright try to write an "actor-proof" and a "director-proof" playscript, as much as it is in his power to do so, while he is actually engaged in the writing of his play. Because after all, that is where the chief authority of playwriting will always reside.

3. THE SCENIC DESIGNER

Scenic designers conceive the physical set for a play, and are responsible for the physical realization of the playscript.

In actual practice, the playwright may never meet the scenic designer; even so, two things need to be said about the playwright's relation to the scenic designer. First, all the necessary indications for a set design should be right there in the playscript text, in minimal stage directions that describe what kind of interior or exterior is needed, and what exits and entrances are needed, and what period, style, or mood is required for the play. All of this is the playwright's responsibility to place in the text itself, to control the physical realization of the play. If a playwright does not put all this in his playscript, then he has no right to complain about a scenic designer who comes along and creates a stage set that is completely inappropriate to what the playwright intended.

Second, the playwright must be aware that every scenic designer has to operate within certain realistic budget considerations. It's easy enough for a playwright to set a scene on the planet Venus, or in an alcove under the Atlantic Ocean, or on top of Mount Everest—it's another thing to expect a fully mounted representation of any of those scenes. Playwrights should remember that Shakespeare wrote all his great plays for a mostly bare stage, where one or two visuals could provide all the setting that was really needed for a play.

Everything we are saying here about scenic designers will apply equally well to sound designers, who have to create any special effects that may be required for the background sound systems of a play.

4. THE LIGHTING DESIGNER

The lighting designer creates the appropriate color, mood, and illumination for a play. As such, he will be particularly concerned with the onstage circumstances of each individual scene—what time of day it is, what season of the year, what the weather is like, etc. And while the playwright may never meet with the lighting designer, even so, the playwright had better put all these specific circumstances into his play text, otherwise the lighting designer may make his own choices and come up with results the playwright did not intend.

In addition to the onstage circumstances of each scene, the lighting designer will also be responsible for any special lighting effects that may be called for in the playscript—flashbacks, sudden blackouts, scene fades, or depictions of special events such as a night sky or a thunder storm or a sudden shift of mood which the director may wish to highlight. Here again, the playwright's best way of controlling these choices will be in the original writing of the playscript, when the playwright himself visualizes how the completed play should appear onstage.

5. THE COSTUME DESIGNER

The costume designer will be responsible for clothing the characters in a play. This may sound simple enough, but the more one thinks about it, the more one realizes this is one of the most crucial aspects of play production: it will involve everything from period and style of costuming, right down to the presentation of the individual characters onstage. And there is no question as to the importance of this most visual side of every production—how can we admire a tragic hero if he is wearing a bizarre costume that is one size too small for him, and if he appears to be of an era that is entirely inappropriate to the action of the play?

A character's clothing will be as revealing of the personality of the character as his make-up is, and in many great plays characters comment on their costumes as part of themselves—Shylock refers to his gabardine, Hamlet refers to his inky cloak, and Lear refers to the "loop'd and window'd raggedness" of the poor creatures that are caught out in the storm on the heath.

And while a playwright may never meet with the costume designer, even so, he had better determine the minimal costume requirements for his characters in the playscript text, otherwise the costume designer may come up with some remarkably original choices—anything from ostrich plumes to frontal nudity. And the playwright will only have himself to blame.

The costume designer will also have to deal with certain special technical problems, such as how many quick costume changes are required within one scene or between scenes, and whether there will be any extraordinarily rough treatment of costumes that will have to be taken into consideration. For example, if a major character has to be stabbed in the last act of a play while he is wearing his full costume, and if it is important that we see streams of blood running all over his costume, does that mean there will have to be a brand new costume for that character for every performance of the play?

These are things that a playwright should train himself to have at the back of his mind as he is writing his play, so he does not introduce impossible conditions for the production of his play.

6. THE PRODUCER

The producer has the responsibility for the mounting and overseeing of the entire production of a play. Depending on the contract that he has with the playwright, the producer may even own the rights to the play itself—which means he will have the right to oversee all parts of the production, from the preliminary casting of actors to the dress rehearsals to the booking of the play on national road companies and leasing it to regional theatres.

This will be a considerable authority on the part of the producer, and it will be one the playwright will have to learn to live with.

In the course of a rehearsal of a play, the producer may feel it is appropriate to cut the total running time of a play, which will mean asking the playwright to exclude a certain quantity of time from the playscript text. Or he may choose to recast certain of the principals or their standbys and understudies, and the playwright may have to be ready to rewrite parts to accommodate these changes. Or sometimes an entire scene will be dropped from a play before its opening, and that will mean the playwright may have to pull in loose ends elsewhere in the play so the omission will not be noticeable. As we say, this is a reality that a playwright may have to learn to live with.

The producer will also control the publicity that will be associated with a play, and here the playwright had better be ready with a single paragraph summary of "what the play is about," or else the press agents will concoct their own version of the play's meaning or message or subject matter, and it may just be light-years away from what the playwright intended.

No matter how frustrating or debilitating the experience of working with a producer may be, it's important always for the playwright to remember that the producer's goal is the same as the playwright's: to have a successful production and run of the play. And hopefully it will be possible to achieve this "success" without compromising the playwright's values or vision of the play itself.

7. THE AUDIENCE

This is what the art of playwriting is all about—the magic of theatre, when a play is presented in full performance before a live audience.

There will be an authentic electricity in the air of any powerful live theatrical performance, and an audience will experience this current and charge in their deepest being. And so will the playwright.

And from a purely technical point of view, there is no better way. In fact, there is really no *other* way to test a playwright's work, the actions and the visuals, than to present them to a live theatre audience.

If these dramatic actions and onstage visuals work well onstage, the playwright will know it because the audience will know it. But if the actions and visuals do not work well onstage, then the playwright will have to try and figure out why they do not communicate strongly to the audience, in order to go on with his work, to modify and strengthen his skills at creating actions and visuals so his next play will work better.

As we said earlier in this book, plays do not really exist until they are performed in front of audiences. That means that the dramatic impulse is really meaningless unless it has some object to receive the original impulse. This is what the art of playwriting is all about.

And of course it's also important to remember that this theatre audience has paid good money to see the play, so there is also a professional obligation to give them the very best theatre experience imaginable.

8. THE DRAMA CRITICS

One has not really been baptized into the theatre until one has seen one's best work impaled on the pen of some drama critic who couldn't write a play to save his own life.

And at times like these, it's important for a playwright to remember that the history of the theatre is littered with just such injustices. Congreve quit writing for the theatre over what happened to *The Way of the World,* and Racine retired from playwriting after the disastrous reception of *Phèdre;* Bizet died broken-hearted over the failure of *Carmen,* and Chekhov died without ever knowing the success of *The Cherry Orchard;* and Edward Albee was denied a Pulitzer Prize for *Who's Afraid of Virginia Woolf?* by the Trustees of Columbia University.

Of course in our own commercial theatre, drama critics and reviews play an inordinate part in the destiny of any play—many a good play has been closed after opening night simply because a few drama critics weren't sharp enough to see why the play was worthwhile. And worse: many a mediocre play has remained open indefinitely simply because a few drama critics weren't perceptive enough to see why the play was not worth keeping on the boards.

So the playwright has to accept the economic reality that reviews *do* matter. But he must also maintain his own inner sanity, and remind himself that reviews do not really have all that much to do with why he is writing plays in the first place. And that is all that really matters in the long run.

* * *

We said at the beginning of this book that the economics of our modern theatre are precarious, and we've all heard stories of how maddening the collaborative work of the theatre can be. But we should also remind ourselves of what we said in the earlier chapters of this book—that the theatre is the most exalted of all art forms, because it is the earliest and the deepest human expression.

Between these two realizations—the necessity to conform to the realities of the marketplace, and the need to preserve the theatre as an exalted art form—the playwright must decide for himself when he should yield to his colleagues on a point of artistic principle, and when he should resist any change in what he has written.

ADVICE FOR PLAYWRIGHTS

Train yourself to see your play from the point of view of the other theatre professionals who will share in the challenge of bringing it to full realization.

SUGGESTED READING

Go back and reread Aristotle's *Poetics,* any edition.

EXERCISES

1. Write a brief scene, and then try to imagine what the following persons would have to say about how to mount this scene onstage: an actor; a director; a producer; an audience.

2. Write a brief scenic and lighting and costume design for the scene you just wrote.

3. Write a brief drama review of the scene you just wrote.

NOTES

PROLOGUE

1. Eugene O'Neill: *A Dramatist's Notebook, The American Spectator,* January 1933.

2. Augustine: *Confessions,* Book Three.

3. Stanislavsky: *My Life In Art* (Meridian, 1948), page 146.

4. Rainer Maria Rilke: *The Notebooks of Malte Laurids Brigge* (Capricorn, 1949), page 196.

5. August Strindberg: Author's Preface to *Miss Julie.*

6. Antonin Artaud: *The Theatre and its Double* (Grove, 1958).

7. Interview with Arthur Miller, *The New York Times,* May 9, 1984.

8. Anton Chekhov: Letter to A. S. Souvorin, 1888.

9. Eugene O'Neill: *A Dramatists Notebook, The American Spectator,* January 1933.

10. David Rabe: *Notes on Sticks and Bones,* 1972.

CHAPTER 1

1. Nathaniel Hawthorne: The Custom-House, Introductory to *The Scarlet Letter*, page 1.
2. James Agee, *The Nation*, 1946.
3. Nathaniel Hawthorne: *The Scarlet Letter*, chapter 24.
4. Shakespeare: *Hamlet*, I, i.
5. Harold Pinter: *The Homecoming*, act I.

CHAPTER 2

1. Tennessee Williams: *The Glass Menagerie*, scene i.
2. Eugene O'Neill: *Long Day's Journey into Night*, act IV.
3. Thornton Wilder: *Our Town*, act III.

CHAPTER 3

1. Richard Boleslavsky: *Acting: The First Six Lessons* (Theatre Arts, 1949).
2. Shakespeare: *Hamlet*, III, ii.
3. Aristotle: Poetics.
4. Shakespeare: *Hamlet*, III, i.
5. Shakespeare: *Macbeth*, I, vii.
6. Shakespeare: *Hamlet*, II, ii.
7. John Webster: *The Duchess of Malfi*, I, i.

CHAPTER 4

1. Uta Hagen: *Respect for Acting* (Macmillan, 1973), page 180.
2. Sophocles: *Oedipus Rex*, translated by David Grene.
3. Shakespeare: *Hamlet*, I, iv.
4. Chekhov: *The Sea Gull*, act IV.

CHAPTER 5

1. Aristotle: *Poetics*.
2. August Strindberg: Author's Preface to *Miss Julie*.

CHAPTER 6

1. A. E. Zucker: *Ibsen, The Master Builder* (Holt, 1929).
2. Eugene O'Neill: *Memoranda on Masks, The American Spectator*, 1932.

CHAPTER 7

1. Sophocles: *Electra*.
2. Shakespeare: *Hamlet*, III, ii.

3. John Osborne: *The Entertainer.*
4. Shakespeare: *Romeo and Juliet,* I, i.
5. Shakespeare: *Macbeth,* V, i.
6. Shakespeare: *Hamlet,* III, i.
7. Shakespeare: *Macbeth,* I, v.
8. Thornton Wilder: *The Matchmaker,* act IV.
9. A. C. Zucker: *Ibsen, The Master Builder* (Holt, 1929).
10. Tennessee Williams, Letter to Audrey Wood, 1939.

CHAPTER 8

1. Thornton Wilder: *The Skin of Our Teeth,* act I.
2. Shakespeare: *The Tempest,* I, ii.
3. Shakespeare: *Henry V,* I, ii.
4. Thornton Wilder: *Our Town,* act I.
5. Edward Albee: *Who's Afraid of Virginia Woolf?,* act I.

CHAPTER 9

1. George Bernard Shaw: Preface to *Three Plays* by Brieux (Brentano's, 1911).
2. Aristotle: *Poetics.*
3. *New York Daily News,* August 14, 1982.
4. Arthur Miller: Introduction to *Collected Plays* (Viking, 1958).

CHAPTER 10

1. Aristotle: *Poetics.*

CHAPTER 12

1. Samuel Beckett: *Waiting for Godot.*
2. Ibid.
3. Eugene Ionesco: *Jack, or The Submission.*
4. Eugene Ionesco: *Rhinoceros.*
5. Ibid.
6. Jean Genet: *The Balcony.*
7. Harold Pinter: *The Caretaker.*
8. Albert Camus: *Caligula.*
9. Beth Henley: *Crimes of the Heart.*
10. Israel Horovitz: *Hopscotch.*
11. Mark Medoff: *The Wager.*
12. David Mamet: *American Buffalo.*

13. David Mamet: *Sexual Perversity in Chicago.*
14. John Ford Noonan: *A Coupla White Chicks Sitting Around Talking.*
15. John Pielmeier: *Agnes of God.*
16. Mark Medoff: *When You Comin' Back, Red Ryder?*
17. Wendy Wasserstein: *Uncommon Women and Others.*
18. William Mastrosimone: *The Woolgatherer.*
19. John Guare: *The House of Blue Leaves.*
20. Miguel Pinero: *Short Eyes.*
21. Sam Shepard: *True West.*
22. Christopher Durang: *Sister Mary Ignatius Explains It All for You.*
23. David Rabe: *The Basic Training of Pavlo Hummel.*
24. David Rabe: *Streamers.*
25. David Rabe: *Sticks and Bones.*
26. David Rabe: *In the Boom Boom Room.*
27. David Berry: *G. R. Point.*
28. Marsha Norman: *Getting Out.*

CHAPTER 13

1. Shakespeare: *Henry V,* V, ii.
2. Ben Jonson: *To the Memory of My Beloved William Shakespeare.*
3. Plato: *Phaedrus.*
4. Aristotle: *Poetics.*
5. Ibid.
6. Stanislavsky: *My Life in Art* (Meridian, 1948).

AFTERWORD

1. Shakespeare: *Hamlet,* III, ii.

APPENDIX

COPYRIGHT, AGENTRY, MARKETING

Following is information on current copyright law, agentry, and marketing that may be useful to the practicing playwright:

Since 1978, current copyright law says a play or musical or work of literature comes under automatic copyright protection as soon as it is created. One can register a playscript with the Copyright Office of the Library of Congress to secure these benefits and to insure remedies against infringements or violations.

One can obtain free copies of "APPLICATION FORM PA" from the Register of Copyrights, Library of Congress, Washington, D. C. 20559. There is a $10 fee for copyrighting a play.

Copyright notice is required on the verso of the title page of a playscript, using the international symbol ©. Duration of copyright for any work created after December 31, 1977, continues for the author's lifetime plus fifty years—unless the work is "made for hire," or anonymous, or pseudononymous, in which case it is seventy-five years from publication, or one hundred years from creation, whichever comes first.

A playwright can always try to get dramatic readings of his work either on his own or through service organizations, such as The New Dramatists Committee, 424 West 44 Street, New York, New York 10036. Most regional theatres have playwriting units and workshops, and most major city universities have drama departments with playwriting divisions.

A playwright can also submit his work to play competitions and contests which are regularly listed in publications such as *The Writer* magazine and *The Dramatists Guild Newsletter*.

As for agentry, one can obtain a listing of agents who handle dramatic materials from The Dramatists Guild, 234 West 44 Street, New York, New York 10036. In submitting a playscript to any of these listed agents, one should always enclose a stamped self-addressed return envelope, and one should also enclose a cover letter giving references and a short biographical resume which includes a history of past productions and publications. Agents will be unlikely to take on any unsolicited material unless one can provide strong credentials and prospects for impending productions.

GLOSSARY OF STAGE TERMS

Following is a brief listing of technical terms that are important in playwriting:

ACTION	What a character wants; his objective.
BEAT	A minor action; a short part of a scene.
CHARACTER	Someone who embodies a major action; someone who wants something.
CLIMAX	A peak of intensity of an action, sometimes occasioning a reversal or discovery.
DENOUEMENT	The final unraveling of the conflict.
DIALOGUE	Rapid back and forth exchange, which advances the action of a play.
DRAMATIC	Showing instead of telling.

161

EXPOSITION

Background material, consisting of prior actions, offstage actions, and given circumstances.

FOURTH WALL

Proscenium arch, for the traditional box set.

GIVEN CIRCUMSTANCES

Whatever impinges on a character in his immediate environment.

MOTIFS

Underlying poetic themes of a play, verbal metaphors or visual emblems.

OBSTACLES

Impediments that prevent a character from getting what he wants.

OFFSTAGE SITUATION

What is going on beyond the immediate reality onstage.

PLOT

The architecture of the major actions of a play.

REVERSAL

"Peripateia" or turning point of an action.

STAKES

How badly someone wants something.

SUBTEXT

Actions which lie beneath the surface dialogue.

THROUGH-LINE

Major subtext action of a play.

VISUAL

Dramatic metaphor that embodies a major action.

CHRONOLOGY OF PLAYS

The following chronology of plays is intended as an ongoing reading list for the practicing playwright. The list contains most of the great plays of Western theatre, from the earliest Greeks on up to the present time, with an opening section on Eastern theatre which contains the titles of representative plays from the Chinese, Japanese, and Indian theatres.

The chronology is loosely arranged in ten historical units with a brief introduction to each period. The units include:

1. Eastern theatre.

2. Greek theatre.

3. Roman theatre.

4. Medieval theatre.

5. Renaissance theatre.

6. Spanish and French theatre.

7. Restoration theatre.

8. Nineteenth century theatre.

9. Modern theatre.

10. Contemporary theatre.

1. EASTERN THEATRE / roughly 2000 years

a. Indian Theatre / circa sixth century B.C.

Early Hindu Vedas contained dialogue and ritual dance and they were sung and acted out by Brahmin priests—Indian plays grew out of these first religious ceremonial pieces, and plays like *The Vision of Vasavadatta* by Bhasa, *The Little Clay Cart* by Shudraka, and *Shakuntala* by Kalidasa, retain this dance and song and poetry of the early Vedas. Perhaps the best introduction to Indian drama is *The King of the Dark Chamber* by the twentieth century Indian dramatist and poet, Rabindranath Tagore, who based his own playwriting on traditional Indian folk legend and ritual.

b. Chinese Theatre / circa 1000 A.D.

Peking Opera is a combination of play, opera, and tumbling acrobatics and ballet. It is unusual pageantry with colorful costumes and unique make-up of white, red, green, and gold face paint. It is the only theatre in the world where one can sit through 17 acts of a play, where each act will recapitulate the action of the previous acts (in case one had to go out for a walk), and where the leading character is sometimes played by two or three separate actors or actresses—one noted for fine acting, one for fine singing, and one for fine acrobatics.

One Peking Opera, *The White Snake,* has its origins back in the Tang Dynasty of 618–907 A.D. It concerns a woman, White Snake, who is an evil demon come down to earth to experience human love—as such, White is dangerous and perverse and the incarnation of everything that men instinctively distrust in the feminine unconscious. The hero of the play, Syu Syan, meets White and her sister Blue during a rainstorm on West Lake, and White contrives to borrow an umbrella from Syu, thus assuming that he will return to her. Syu and White agree to wed, and White gives Syu some stolen money to arrange the wedding—but Syu is arrested and exiled, and he is still not sure whether White is a benign spirit or a pernicious demon. Finally a Taoist priest, Fa Hai, confronts White, but she beats him back and overcomes him.

It is a curious story and has gone through several versions, the most recent of which appeared after the Cultural Revolution in China in 1949, when Mao Tse Tung had the play rewritten by Tyan Han to reflect modern communist values. An English version of this Han text was performed in 1972 at the Institute for Advanced Studies in the Theatre Arts in New York, and is published in *The Red Pear Garden* by David Godine, Boston.

c. Japanese Theatre / circa 1336 A.D.

Of the three forms of Japanese theatre—Noh, Kabuki, and doll theatre—the Noh is by far the most highly stylized. It is a slow motion dance theatre with spoken lines deeply intoned by actors according to a set inflection. Noh is governed by the principle of *yūgen* (yer-gen), which is an indecipherable quality and discipline that is as elusive to a westerner as zen. One translator, Arthur Waley, tries to describe yūgen as follows: "What lies beneath the surface; the subtle as opposed to the obvious; the hint, as opposed to the statement."

Noh was originated in the fifteenth century by Seami Motokiyo, and one of the earliest Noh plays is *Ikkaku Sennin* by Komparu Zembō Motayasu (1453–1532). It is a dragon play, magical and haunting in its autumn imagery, subtle and poignant in its sense of time and loss, yet surprising in its sense of release and restoration. Ikkaku Sennin is a holy hermit unicorn who has captured the dragon gods who cause rain, and he has kept them hidden away so there is a terrible drought in the land.

An English version of this play was performed at the Institute for Advanced Studies in the Theatre Arts in New York in 1964, and is published by Hill and Wang in *Classic Asian Plays*.

2. GREEK THEATRE / fifth century B.C.

The Greek theatre was at its height during the course of two major wars—the Persian War (490–470 B.C.), and the Peloponnesian Wars (431–404 B.C.). Every major Greek city or polis had its own amphitheatre where the plays were staged, usually during festivals dedicated to the god Dionysos.

a. Aeschylus 525–456 B.C.
90 plays, 7 of which are extant:

Agamemnon
Choephori
Eumenides
The Persians
The Suppliant Maidens
The Seven Against Thebes
Prometheus Bound

b. Sophocles 495–405 B.C.
120 plays, 7 of which are extant:

Philoctetes
Electra
Ajax
Women of Trachis
Oedipus Rex
Antigone
Oedipus at Colonus

c. Euripides 480–406 B.C.
80–90 plays, 18 of which are extant:

Medea
Ion
Hippolytus
Heracleidae
The Cyclops
Rhesus
Alcestis
Heracles
Hecuba
The Trojan Women
Iphigenia in Tauris
Iphigenia in Aulis
Helen
Electra
Orestes
Andromache
The Suppliant Women
The Phoenician Women
The Bacchae

d. Aristophanes 448–380 B.C.
11 plays are extant:

The Knights
The Clouds
The Wasps
Peace
The Birds
Acharnians
Lysistrata
Thesmophariozusae
The Frogs
Ecclesiazusae
Plutus

e. Menander 342–292 B.C.
100 plays, 3 of which are extant:

The Girl From Samos
Arbitration
Sharing of Glycera

3. ROMAN THEATRE / circa 2000 years old

The Roman theatre was more of a popular spectacle than the Greek theatre was, partly because the Romans borrowed their religion from the Greeks but obviously did not take the great mythic figures as seriously as the Greeks did. Therefore their plays tended more towards theatricality and immediate effect. Seneca modeled all his tragedies after Greek plays, sometimes with monstrous consequences.

a. Plautus 254–184 B.C.
130 plays, 21 of which are extant:

Amphitryo
Menaechmi
Aulularia
Bacchides
Captivi
Mostellaria
Miles Gloriosus
Pseudolus
Rudens
Trinummus

Asinaria
Casina
Cistellaria
Curculio
Epidicus
Mercator
Persa
Poenulus
Stichus
Truculentus
Viduliaria

b. Terence 190–159 B.C.
6 plays are extant:

Andria
Hecyra
Heauton Timorumenos
Eunuchus
Phormio
Adelphoe

c. Seneca 3 B.C.–65 A.D.
9 plays are extant:

Phaedra
Medea
Hercules Furens
Troades
Agamemnon
Oedipus
Hercules Oetaeus
Phoenissae
Thyestes

4. MEDIEVAL THEATRE / circa 1300–1450 A.D.

The theatre of the Middle Ages grew out of roving troupes of mimes and acrobats and jugglers and troubadours, and also out of the public spectacles of church processions and executions and tournaments. Later, pageant wagons presented plays that were prepared in trade guilds by anonymous authors. There are four surviving cycles of plays—the York cycle, the Towneley cycle, the N. Town cycle, and the Chester plays.

The chief plays that can be dated include:

1150   *Adam*

1264   The Corpus Christi Festival is revived and Nativity plays are put on, which grow into the later miracle plays and mystery plays and morality plays.

1425   *The Second Shepherds Play*

1475   *Everyman*

One of the best examples of Medieval theatre is *The Second Shepherds Play*—which has nothing to do with a second shepherd, it is simply the second of two Shepherd plays that were put on as part of the Wakefield plays.

The Second Shepherds Play is filled with the raucous, bawdy, coarse animal spirits that we associate with the paintings of Breughel, and this earthy, peasant-like, festive spirit grows quite naturally and miraculously into the announcement of the birth of the Christ child, and the play ends with sublime images of chastity and immaculate conception and nativity.

5. RENAISSANCE THEATRE / circa 1500–1700 A.D.

With humanism and the explosion of interest in history and psychology and geography, the Renaissance theatre was enormously influenced by the *commedia dell'arte* of Italy where characters were all seen as archetypes and one actor could play a single role for his entire lifetime, inventing endless variations as the dramatic situations changed. This resilience was just what was needed for the development of a rigorous Renaissance theatre in all its later forms.

Following is a chronology of the major plays of the English Renaissance:

1552   *Gammer Gurton's Needle*

1586   Thomas Kyd: *The Spanish Tragedy*

1587   Christopher Marlowe: *Tamburlaine*

1589   Christopher Marlowe: *Doctor Faustus*

1590   Christopher Marlowe: *Edward II*

1592   Christopher Marlowe: *The Jew of Malta*

William Shakespeare: *Henry VI*
Richard III
A Comedy of Errors

1593   William Shakespeare: *Titus Andronicus*
The Taming of the Shrew

1594   William Shakespeare: *Two Gentlemen of Verona*
Love's Labour's Lost
Romeo and Juliet

1595   William Shakespeare: *Richard II*
A Midsummer Night's Dream

1596   William Shakespeare: *King John*
The Merchant of Venice

1597   William Shakespeare: *Henry IV* parts i & ii

1598   Ben Jonson: *Every Man in His Humour*

William Shakespeare: *Much Ado About Nothing*
As You Like It
Twelfth Night
Julius Caesar
Henry V

1600   Thomas Dekker: *The Shoemaker's Holiday*

1601   William Shakespeare: *Hamlet*
The Merry Wives of Windsor

1602   William Shakespeare: *All's Well that Ends Well*
Troilus and Cressida

1603   Ben Jonson: *Sejanus*

1604   William Shakespeare: *Measure for Measure*
Othello

1605   Ben Jonson: *Volpone*

William Shakespeare: *King Lear*
Macbeth

1606   William Shakespeare: *Antony and Cleopatra*

1607   William Shakespeare: *Coriolanus*
Timon of Athens

1608   William Shakespeare: *Pericles*

1609   William Shakespeare: *Cymbeline*

1610   Ben Jonson: *The Alchemist*

William Shakespeare: *The Winter's Tale*

1611   John Webster: *The White Devil*

William Shakespeare: *The Tempest*

1613   John Webster: *The Duchess of Malfi*

William Shakespeare: *Henry VIII*

1614   Ben Jonson: *Bartholomew Fair*

1619   Beaumont and Fletcher: *The Maid's Tragedy*

1623   Thomas Middleton: *The Changeling*

1633   John Ford: *'Tis Pity She's a Whore*

1634   Fletcher: *The Two Noble Kinsmen*

6. THE SPANISH AND FRENCH THEATRES / circa 1580–1726

a. The Spanish Theatre

The Spanish Renaissance took place in the Counter-Reformation, in a country that still had a feudal culture with Moorish and Jewish foundations, and with expansionist activities going on in Peru and Mexico and America.

The so-called "Golden Age of Spanish Theatre" has been characterized as "capa y spada"—cape and sword—something akin to our concept of swashbuckling and chivalric codes.

There are three major playwrights of this period: Tirso de Molina (1570–1648), the creator of the Don Juan legend; Lope de Vega (1562–1635) who wrote over 2000 plays, mostly melodramas like *The Knight From Olmeda*—Lope survived the defeat of the Spanish Armada in 1588 and ended as an informer to the infamous Spanish Inquisition; and Calderón de la Barca (1600–1681), who wrote poetic and philosophical plays including *La Dama Duende* and *La Vida Es Sueña*.

b. The French Theatre

The French theatre in its Neoclassic Renaissance was elegant and polished in the same way the court of Louis XIV was elegant and polished—it was this Sun King who built the elaborate palace of Versailles, who said "L'état, c'est moi," and who insisted on a spirit of "politesse" which was an infinite courtliness and surface courtesy. Out of this ritualistic society came La Fontaine with his fables, and the plays of Corneille (1606–1684), Molière (1622–1673), Racine (1639–1699), Beaumarchais (1732–1799), and Marivaux (1688–1763).

Following are the major plays of this French theatre:

1636	Corneille: *The Cid*
1659	Molière: *Les Precieuses Ridicules*
1662	Molière: *L'école des Femmes*
1664	Molière: *Tartuffe*
1665	Molière: *Don Juan*
1666	Molière: *Le Misanthrope*
	Le Médicin Malgre Lui
1667	Racine: *Andromaque*
1668	Molière: *Amphitryon*
	L'Avare
1669	Racine: *Britannicus*
1670	Molière: *Le Bourgeois Gentilhommes*
	Les Femmes Savantes
	Le Malade Imaginaire
1677	Racine: *Phèdre*
1726	Marivaux: *Les Fausses Confidences*

7. THE RESTORATION THEATRE / 1660–1777

During the Puritan Revolution in England (1642–1660), many English aristocrats fled to Europe where they frequented the French theatre, and this accounts in large part for the comedy of manners that developed in the theatre of the Restoration, after Charles II reclaimed the English throne. These plays were mostly prose satires on middle class values, urbane and mercurial domestic intrigues; the stakes rarely rose any higher than who would get to have a liason with whom, and when, and how, and where, and why.

Following are the major plays of the Restoration:

1700	William Congreve: *The Way of the World*
1707	George Farquhar: *The Beaux Strategem*
1728	John Gay: *The Beggar's Opera*
1773	Oliver Goldsmith: *She Stoops to Conquer*
1775	Richard Brinsley Sheridan: *The Rivals*
1777	Richard Brinsley Sheridan: *The School For Scandal*

8. THE NINETEENTH CENTURY THEATRE / 1800–1899

A revolutionary era produced revolutionary playwrights—chief among them the Norwegian Henrik Ibsen, whose plays of social criticism stirred the world out of its conventional archetypes and enforced new thinking about men, women, marriage, and hereditary patterns. The Swedish August Strindberg also forged a dynamic new theatre of dark psychological drama in which the power struggle between male and female was depicted with stunning fury. The Russian Anton Chekhov wrote a consummate drama that portrayed a dying Czarist order, and a vague sense of the descent of modernism—for better or for worse.

Following are the major works of this nineteenth century theatre:

1830	Victor Hugo: *Hernani*
1838	Victor Hugo: *Ruy Blas*
1866	Ibsen: *Brand*
1867	Ibsen: *Peer Gynt*
1873	Ibsen: *The Emperor and the Galilean*
1877	Ibsen: *The Pillars of Society*
1879	Ibsen: *A Doll's House*
1881	Ibsen: *Ghosts*
1882	Ibsen: *An Enemy of the People*
1884	Ibsen: *The Wild Duck*
1886	Tolstoy: *The Power of Darkness*
	Ibsen: *Rosmersholm*
1887	Strindberg: *The Father*
1888	Strindberg: *Miss Julie*
	Comrades
	Ibsen: *The Lady From the Sea*
1891	Ibsen: *Hedda Gabler*
1892	Ibsen: *The Master Builder*
1893	Shaw: *Mrs. Warren's Profession*
1894	Ibsen: *Little Eyolf*
	Shaw: *Arms and the Man*
1895	Oscar Wilde: *The Importance of Being Earnest*
1896	Strindberg: *The Creditors*
	Chekhov: *The Sea Gull*
	Ibsen: *John Gabriel Borkman*
1897	Rostand: *Cyrano de Bergerac*
	Chekhov: *Uncle Vanya*
1898	Shaw: *Caesar and Cleopatra*
	Strindberg: *To Damascus*

1900	Chekhov: *The Three Sisters*
	Strindberg: *The Dance of Death*
	Ibsen: *When We Dead Awaken*
1901	Strindberg: *A Dream Play*
	The Dance of Death
1903	Gorky: *The Lower Depths*
1904	Chekhov: *The Cherry Orchard*
1907	Strindberg: *A Ghost Sonata*

9. THE MODERN THEATRE / 1900–1990

After the revolutionary plays of the nineteenth century, the theatre settled down to explore the bewilderments and contradictions of a world that had been deeply shaken by the work of Darwin, Marx, Einstein, and Freud.

George Bernard Shaw wrote plays that were filled with adroit dialogue, masterful stagecraft, and acid skepticism—he created a modern comedy that exalted the outcome of certain inevitable historical forces. Luigi Pirandello developed a prismatic, intellectual, querulous theatre where dramatic form itself kept becoming its own major action.

In America, plays began to emerge from certain theatre groups— the Washington Square Players, the Provincetown Players, Eva LeGallienne's Civic Repertory Theatre, the Jewish Workers' Theatre, and the Mercury Theatre of Orson Welles. More than any other American playwright, Eugene O'Neill pioneered an American theatre that was based on his own life experience and an extensive reading of the works of Freud, so that O'Neill tried to create plays that would trace the unconscious actions of their major characters.

Following are some of the major plays of the modern theatre:

1903	Shaw: *Man and Superman*
1905	Shaw: *Major Barbara*
1906	Shaw: *The Doctor's Dilemma*
1907	Synge: *The Playboy of the Western World*
1910	Shaw: *The Dark Lady of the Sonnets*
1912	Shaw: *Androcles and the Lion*
1913	Shaw: *Pygmalion*
1919	Shaw: *Heartbreak House*
1920	O'Neill: *The Emperor Jones*
	Shaw: *Back to Methuselah*
1921	O'Neill: *The Hairy Ape*
	Pirandello: *Six Characters in Search of an Author*

1923   O'Neill: *Marco Millions*
             All God's Chillun Got Wings
        Shaw: *Saint Joan*
1924   O'Neill: *Desire Under the Elms*
        Kaufman & Connelly: *Beggar on Horseback*
1925   O'Neill: *The Great God Brown*
             Lazarus Laughed
1926   O'Neill: *Strange Interlude*
1929   Elmer Rice: *Street Scene*
1930   Marc Connelly: *Green Pastures*
        Noel Coward: *Private Lives*
1931   O'Neill: *Mourning Becomes Electra*
        Shaw: *Too True to Be Good*
        Wilder: *The Short Happy Journey to Trenton and Camden*
1933   Lorca: *Blood Wedding*
        Brecht: *The Threepenny Opera*
1934   Hellman: *The Children's Hour*
1935   Lorca: *Yerma*
        T. S. Eliot: *Murder in the Cathedral*
        Odets: *Awake and Sing!*
1936   Lorca: *The House of Bernarda Alba*
        Anderson: *Winterset*
1937   Brecht: *Galileo*
        Williams: *The Fugitive Kind*
1938   Wilder: *Our Town*
        Brecht: *The Good Woman of Setzuan*
1939   Wilder: *The Merchant of Yonkers*
        Hellman: *The Little Foxes*
        Saroyan: *The Time of Your Life*
1940   Williams: *Battle of Angels*
1941   Brecht: *Mother Courage*
        Hellman: *Watch on the Rhine*
        O'Neill: *Long Day's Journey into Night* (produced 1946)
        Noel Coward: *Blithe Spirit*
1942   Giraudoux: *The Apollo of Belloc*
        Wilder: *The Skin of Our Teeth*
1943   Sartre: *The Flies*
1944   Anouilh: *Antigone*
        Williams: *The Glass Menagerie*
        Miller: *The Man Who Had All the Luck*
1945   Giraudoux: *The Madwoman of Chaillot*
        O'Neill: *The Iceman Cometh*
1946   Williams: *27 Wagons Full of Cotton*
        Hellman: *Another Part of the Forest*
1947   Williams: *A Streetcar Named Desire*
        Miller: *All My Sons*

1948	Williams: *Summer and Smoke*
	Christopher Fry: *The Lady's Not For Burning*
1949	Miller: *Death of a Salesman*
	T. S. Eliot: *The Cocktail Party*
	Williams: *This Property Is Condemned*
1950	Ionesco: *The Bald Soprano*
1951	Christopher Fry: *A Sleep of Prisoners*
	Williams: *The Rose Tattoo*
1953	Miller: *The Crucible*
	Williams: *Camino Real*
	Samuel Beckett: *Waiting for Godot*
1954	Wilder: *The Matchmaker*
1955	Williams: *Cat on a Hot Tin Roof*
	Miller: *A View From the Bridge*
	A Memory of Two Mondays
1957	John Osborne: *The Entertainer*
1959	Williams: *Sweet Bird of Youth*
1960	Genet: *The Balcony*
	Ionesco: *Rhinoceros*
	Pinter: *The Caretaker*
1961	Williams: *The Night of the Iguana*
1962	Albee: *Who's Afraid of Virginia Woolf?*
	Beckett: *Happy Days*
1964	Miller: *After the Fall*
1965	Pinter: *The Homecoming*
1966	Peter Weiss: *Marat/Sade*
1967	Beckett: *Endgame*
1968	Pinter: *No Man's Land*

10. THE CONTEMPORARY THEATRE

In 1950, Actors Equity laid down rules for performances in 199 and 299 seat houses in New York, theatres that were outside the commercial midtown area, and as a consequence the "off-Broadway" theatre movement was made legal and a part of the ongoing dramatic experience of American playwriting. Off-Broadway offered a vigorous, alternative theatre that was experimental, non-commercial, and devoted to exploring the possibilities of staging whatever kind of plays seemed relevant to the contemporary world.

During this era, Joseph Papp won his battle to produce free Shakespeare in Central Park, and later opened his Public Theatre downtown in Manhattan. Numerous theatre groups sprang into existence, like the Judson Church which put on a production of Gertrude Stein's *In Circles,* adapted by Al Carmines and Larry Kornfeld; Tom Eyen and his Theatre of the Eye, produced such plays as *The White Whore and the Bit Player*. There were companies that grew out of specific theatre locations such as the Phoenix and the Circle in the Square, and there were significant revivals of classic plays like William Ball's *Six Characters In Search of an Author* by Pirandello, and José Quintero's *The Iceman Cometh* by O'Neill.

Special mention should be made here of the renewal of interest in the one act play form—Edward Albee's *The Zoo Story*, *The Death of Bessie Smith*, and *The American Dream;* Leroi Jones' *Dutchman*, *The Slave*, and *The Toilet;* Michael McClure's *The Beard;* and Samuel Beckett's *Krapp's Last Tape* and *Endgame*.

Perhaps the best way of representing the outstanding plays of this contemporary theatre, is to set down in alphabetical order a selective checklist of recommended playwrights and plays—which the reader can keep as an ongoing record, adding his own choices of authors and play titles to the following list:

Kenneth H. Brown: *The Brig*

Caryl Churchill: *Cloud 9*
Fen
Top Girls

Rosalyn Drexler: *Transients Welcome*
Home Movies

Christopher Durang: *Sister Mary Ignatius Explains it All to You*
Beyond Therapy

Lonnie Elder: *Ceremonies in Dark Old Men*

Jules Feiffer: *Grownups*
Little Murders

Harvey Fierstein: *Torch Song Trilogy*
La Cage Aux Folles

Maria Irene Fornes: *Mud*
The Danube
The Conduct of Life
Promenade

Paul Foster: *Tom Paine*

Bruce Jay Friedman: *Steambath*

Jack Gelber: *The Connection*
The Apple

Jean Genet: *The Blacks*
The Balcony

Frank Gilroy: *Who'll Save the Plowboy?*
    The Subject Was Roses

John Guare: *Cop Out*
    House of Blue Leaves

Charles Gordone: *No Place to Be Somebody*

Peter Handke: *Kasper*

Lorraine Hansberry: *A Raisin in the Sun*
    The Sign in Sidney Brustein's Window
    To Be Young, Gifted, and Black

Ronald Harwood: *The Dresser*

Beth Henley: *Crimes of the Heart*

Venable Herndon: *Until the Monkey Comes*

Richard Hoffman: *Modern Times*
    The Seekers

Israel Horovitz: *Line*
    The Indian Wants the Bronx
    Hopscotch

Tina Howe: *Painting Churches*

Eugene Ionesco: *Rhinoceros*
    Jack
    The Bald Soprano

Jean-Claude Van Itallie: *America Hurrah*
    The Serpent
    Baglady

James Kirkwood: *A Chorus Line*

Arthur Kopit: *Oh Dad, Poor Dad, Mama's Hung You in the Closet*
    and I'm Feelin' So Sad
    Indians
    Wings

Ira Levin: *Death Trap*

Romulus Linney: *Just Folks*
    Laughing Stock

David Mamet: *American Buffalo*
    Sexual Perversities in Chicago
    Glenn Gary, Glenn Ross
    Reunion
    Dark Pony

Mark Medoff: *When You Comin' Back, Red Ryder?*
      Children of a Lesser God

William Mastrosimone: *Extremities*

Leonard Melfi: *Butterfaces*
      Birdbath
      Halloween
      Ferryboat

Jason Miller: *That Championship Season*

Tad Mosel: *All the Way Home*

Peter Nichols: *A Day in the Death of Joe Egg*

John Ford Noonan: *A Coupla White Chicks Sittin Around Talkin*

Marsha Norman: *'Night, Mother*
      Getting Out
      Traveler in the Dark

Rochelle Owens: *Chucky's Hunch*
      Futz
      The Karl Marx Play

Robert Patrick: *Kennedy's Children*

John Pielmeier: *Agnes of God*

Miguel Pinero: *Short Eyes*

David Rabe: *Streamers*
      Sticks and Bones
      Hurlyburly

Jack Richardson: *The Prodigal*

Peter Shaffer: *Equus*
      Amadeus

Ntozake Shange: *For Colored Girls Who Have Considered Suicide*
      When The Rainbow is Enuf

Sam Shepard: *Buried Child*
      Fool For Love
      True West
      Curse of the Starving Class
      The Tooth of Crime

Neil Simon: *Barefoot in the Park*
      The Odd Couple
      Plaza Suite

Brighton Beach Memoirs
Biloxi Blues

Tom Stoppard: *The Real Thing*
Rosencrantz and Guildenstern Are Dead
Travesties

Elizabeth Swados: *Runaways*

Ronald Tavel: *Gorilla Queen*

Megan Terry: *Viet Rock*
The Gloaming, Oh My Darling

Douglas Turner Ward: *Day of Absence*
Happy Ending

Wendy Wasserstein: *Uncommon Women and Others*

Michael Weller: *Moonchildren*
Loose Ends

Peter Weiss: *Marat/Sade*
The Investigation

Lanford Wilson: *Hot L Baltimore*
Tally's Folly
Balm in Gilead
Home Free

Paul Zindel: *The Effect of Gamma Rays on Man-in-the-moon Marigolds*

SELECTED BIBLIOGRAPHY

Following is a listing of books that are especially recommended to the practicing playwright:

Aristotle: *Poetics* (any edition).
Antonin Artaud: *The Theatre and Its Double.* Grove Press, 1958.
Toby Cole: *Playwrights on Playwriting.* Dramabook, 1961.
Uta Hagen: *Respect for Acting.* Macmillan, 1973.
Friedrich Nietzsche: *The Birth of Tragedy* (any edition).
Constantin Stanislavsky: *My Life in Art.* Meridian, 1948.
Tennessee Williams: *Memoirs.* Doubleday, 1972.

Following is a listing of books that are also recommended for some particular aspect of plays and playwriting:

William Archer: *Playmaking—A Manual of Craftsmanship.* Dodd, Mead, 1928.

George Pierce Baker: *Dramatic Technique.* Houghton Mifflin, 1918.

Jean-Louis Barrault: *The Theatre of Jean-Louis Barrault.* Theatre Arts, 1946.

Bernard Beckerman: *Dynamics of Drama.* Drama Book Specialists, 1970.

Richard Boleslavsky: *Acting: The First Six Lessons.* Theatre Arts, 1949.

Dorothea Brande: *Becoming a Writer.* Houghton Mifflin, 1981.

Harold Clurman: *The Fervent Years.* Di Capo, 1945.

Lajos Egri: *The Art of Dramatic Writing.* Simon & Schuster, 1978.

Francis Fergusson: *The Idea of a Theatre.* Princeton, 1949.

Ann Folke and Richard Harden: *Opportunities in Theatrical Design and Production.* VGM National Textbook Company, 1983.

John Gassner: *Masters of the Drama.* Random House, 1954.

Bernard Grebanier: *Playwriting.* Barnes & Noble, 1979.

John Howard Lawson: *The Theory and Technique of Playwriting.* Hill & Wang, 1960.

Moses Malvinsky: *The Science of Playwriting.* Coward-McCann, Inc., 1979.

John D. Mitchell: *Theatre: The Search for Style.* Northwood Institute Press, 1982.

George Polti: *The 36 Dramatic Situations.* The Writer, Inc., 1981.

Kenneth Thorpe Rowe: *Write That Play.* Minerva Press, 1968.

Michel St. Denis: *Theatre: The Rediscovery of Style.* Theatre Arts, 1960.

John van Druten: *Playwrights at Work.* Harper and Bros., 1953.

1. Aristotle's *Poetics*. Fill in the blank spaces in the following excerpts from the *Poetics:*

> Tragedy, then, is an _____ of an _____ that is _____, complete, and of a certain _____; in _____ embellished with each kind of artistic ornament, the several kinds being found in separate parts of the play; in the form of _____, not of _____; through _____ and _____ effecting the proper _____ of these emotions.
>
> • • • • • •
>
> The _____, though an attraction, is the least artistic of all the parts, and has least to do with the art of poetry.
>
> • • • • • •

As far as may be, too, the poet should even ———————————— his story with the very ———————————— of his personages; given the same natural qualifications, he who feels the ———————————— to be described will be the most convincing . . .

• • • • • •

It is evident from the above that the poet must be more the poet of his ———————————— or ———————————— than of his verses, inasmuch as he is a poet by virtue of the ———————————— element in his work, and it is ———————————— that he imitates.

• • • • • •

2. MATCHING QUIZ.

Put the correct letter in the blank next to its appropriate answer:

a. ACTION ——————— the final unraveling of the conflict
b. DENOUEMENT ——————— what a character wants
c. PLOT ——————— impediment in the way of action
d. OBSTACLE ——————— architecture of major actions
e. EXPOSITION ——————— peak of intensity of action
f. MOTIF ——————— necessary background material
g. REVERSAL ——————— underlying poetic theme
h. CLIMAX ——————— how badly someone wants something
i. STAKES ——————— a turning of an action

• • • • • •

Put the correct letter in the blank next to its appropriate answer:

a. AESCHYLUS ——————— wrote *The Zoo Story*
b. EURIPEDES ——————— wrote *Mother Courage*
c. SHAKESPEARE ——————— wrote *Le Misanthrope*
d. BEN JONSON ——————— wrote *Phèdre*
e. RACINE ——————— wrote *Boom*
f. MOLIERE ——————— wrote *Twelfth Night*
g. EDWARD ALBEE ——————— wrote *Every Man in His Humour*
h. TENNESSEE WILLIAMS ——————— wrote *Agamemnon*
i. BERTOLT BRECHT ——————— wrote *Medea*

• • • • • •

Put the correct letter in the blank next to its appropriate answer:

a. WILLY LOMAN ——————— in *Hamlet*
b. STANLEY KOWALSKI ——————— in *The Caretaker*
c. LAERTES ——————— in *The Matchmaker*

d. AMANDA WINGFIELD   _____ in *Oedipus Rex*
e. DOLLY LEVI   _____ in *Macbeth*
f. JOCASTA   _____ in *The Sea Gull*
g. TRIGORIN   _____ in *A Streetcar Named Desire*
h. DAVIES   _____ in *Death of a Salesman*
i. MALCOLM   _____ in *The Glass Menagerie*

• • • • • •

Put the correct letter in the blank next to its appropriate answer:

a. CLASSICAL THEATRE   _____ *Phèdre*
b. ROMAN THEATRE   _____ *Futz*
c. MEDIEVAL THEATRE   _____ *She Stoops to Conquer*
d. RENAISSANCE THEATRE   _____ *The Trojan Women*
e. JACOBEAN THEATRE   _____ *Hedda Gabler*
f. NEOCLASSIC THEATRE   _____ *The Second Shepherds Play*
g. RESTORATION THEATRE
h. NINETEENTH CENTURY THEATRE   _____ *The Duchess of Malfi*
i. CONTEMPORARY THEATRE   _____ *Henry V*
  _____ *Phaedra*

3. MULTIPLE CHOICE

Circle the correct letter next to the most appropriate answer:

The designation DSR refers to that part of the stage that is:

a. in the back and to the actor's left
b. in the front and to the actor's left
c. in the front and to the actor's right

Aristotle says the tragic deed should be:

a. within the body politic
b. within the family
c. within the playwright's head

The difference between narrative and dramatic is:

a. the first tells and the second shows
b. the first shows and the second tells
c. the first tells and the second describes

The leading actor in Shakespeare's company was:

a. Edward Alleyne
b. Will Kempe
c. Richard Burbage

Goethe spent the following time period writing *Faust:*

a. 6 months
b. 6 years
c. 60 years

Lope de Vega wrote a total of:
a. 15–20 plays
b. 1500–2000 plays
c. 15000–20000 plays

The working title of *Summer and Smoke* was:
a. *Winter and Cigarettes*
b. *A Chart of Anatomy*
c. *The Poker Night*

The Roman theatre included Seneca, Plautus, and:
a. Sappho
b. Terence
c. Cicero

The Restoration theatre included Sheridan, Congreve, and:
a. Marlowe
b. Goldsmith
c. Corneille

Ibsen spent two years working on:
a. *A Doll's House*
b. *The Dance of Death*
c. *Miss Julie*

Gozzi said there could only be thirty-six:
a. performances of a play
b. plots for a play
c. actors in a play

Chekhov thought Stanislavsky's direction of *The Sea Gull* was:
a. competent
b. terrific
c. disastrous

Antonin Artaud advocated a:
a. theatre of kindness
b. theatre of cruelty
c. theatre of irony

Brecht trained his actors to express:
    a. direct identification with their parts
    b. alienation from their parts
    c. typecasting

"Don't write a play; write plays" was said by:
    a. Tennessee Williams
    b. Anton Chekhov
    c. Ben Jonson

Plato said the one prerequisite for being an artist was:
    a. talent
    b. training
    c. madness

4. IDENTIFICATION

Identify the *title* and *author* and *character speaking* for each of the following quotations:

Well, up to a year ago I used to like you a lot. And I used to watch you as you did everything . . . because we'd been friends so long . . . and then you began spending all your time at *baseball* . . . and you never stopped to speak to anybody anymore.

Astride of a grave and a difficult birth. Down in the hole, lingeringly, the gravedigger puts on the forceps. We have time to grow old.

I was driving along, you understand? And I was fine. I was even observing the scenery. You can imagine, me looking at scenery, on the road every week of my life.

I play so badly now. I'm all out of practice. Sister Theresa will give me a dreadful scolding. She'll tell me it isn't fair to my father when he spends so much money for extra lessons. She's quite right, it isn't fair . . .

What was I talking about? . . . Yes, about the stage. I'm not like that now. Now I am a real actress. I act with intense enjoyment, with enthusiasm; on the stage I am intoxicated and I feel that I am beautiful. But now, while I'm living here, I go for walks a lot. I keep walking and thinking . . .

Money, I've always felt, money—pardon my expression—is like manure; it's not worth a thing unless it's spread about encouraging young things to grow.

When you get down to bone, you haven't got all the way, yet. There's something inside the bone . . . the marrow . . . and that's what you gotta get at.

When I am thirty, she will be forty-five. When I am sixty, she will be seventy-five.

Let you not mistake your duty as I mistook my own. I came into this village like a bridegroom to his beloved, bearing gifts of high religion; the very crown of holy law I brought, and what I touched with my bright confidence, it died . . .

Yeah, this angry, petulant old man. I mean He's represented like a bad-tempered childish old, old, sick, peevish man—I mean like the sort of old man in a nursing home that's putting together a jigsaw puzzle and can't put it together and gets furious at it and kicks over the table.

God grant us rest from labour! A long year I have kept this vigil, lying with pricked ear, As a dog lies, above the Atreidae's hall . . .

King Phoebus in plain words commanded us to drive out a pollution from our land . . .

How are you, honey? How is that kidney condition? *Horrors!* You're a Christian martyr, yes, honey, that's what you are, a Christian martyr!

When Oswald came in at that door with the pipe in his mouth, I thought for a moment it was his father in the flesh.

George who is out there somewhere there in the dark . . . George who is good to me, and whom I revile; who understands me, and whom I push off; who can make me laugh, and I choke it back in my throat; who can hold me, at night, so that it's warm, and whom I will bite so there's blood; who keeps learning the games we play as quickly as I can change the rules; who can make me happy and I do not wish to be happy, and yes I do wish to be happy . . .

That's maybe why I came; I think I still believe it. That underneath we're all profoundly friends! I can't believe this world; all this hatred isn't real to me!

I've been aboard this destroyer for two weeks now and we've already been through four air attacks. I'm in the war at last, Doc. I've caught up with that task force that passed me by. I'm glad to be here. I had to be here, I guess . . .

Well, to sum up, everything was in my favour, for a killing. Don't worry about the chauffeur. The chauffeur would never have spoken. He was an old friend of the family. But . . . in the end I thought . . . Aaah, why go to all the bother . . . you know, getting rid of the corpse and all that, getting yourself into a state of tension. So I just gave her another belt in the nose and a couple of turns of the boot and sort of left it at that . . .

Oh words, what crimes are committed in your name!

INDEX

M4b